Donald Trump: Crazy or Genius?

Learn How to Win from Your Enemy

Hassan Farhangi

Donald Trump: Crazy or Genius?
Learn How to Win from Your Enemy

Darya Publication
London
September 2024

Written by
Hassan Farhangi

Contents

Book one .... **Error! Bookmark not defined.**
    Introduction 1
    Exploring the Depths of "Dad" and "Father" 4
    What is success? 13
    Cognitive Impairment Due to External Factors 16
    The Power of Belief 22
    To surrender or not to surrender 23
    Stop reading 35

Summary 36
Activity 38
The trap of doubt 41
    The Eagle with a Broken Wing 41
    Toxic Beliefs 43
    Ineffective words produce negative emotions 47
    The effect of negative words on behaviour 48
    Why Trump 50

Activity: 52
Book Two 57
Chapter 1 58
The power 58
    Power is not inherent but acquired 59
    Self-power of an ant 73
    Lions die without eating food! 79
    Having financial stability is necessary 79
    Know What You Want! 86
    Wanting is not enough; ask and take a step! 86
    The lion licks its wounds and continues onward 92
    Controllable and uncontrollable challenges 92
    The limitations of human control 99
    Lions do not become cats by mocking 107

  The Angry Lion Only Hurts 110

  The lion also dies 116

  Everything is mortal 116

Chapter Summary 118

Chapter 2 121

Wanting 121

  Reboot your brain 123

  Are you a lion or a fox? Make a decision! 126

  Do you prefer poverty or wealth? 128

  Understanding Our Desires: Exploring the Path to Prosperity . 130

  Double standards are the enemy of successful 132

  Believe in abundance 137

  Do you attract wealth or poverty? 139

  Characteristics of optimistic individuals: 145

  Having a clear and accurate view of yourself: 145

  Characteristics of pessimistic individuals: 159

  Chapter Summary 173

Chapter 3 176

Methods 177

  Rereading technique 180

  SPEAR Techniques 181

  SMART Techniques 188

  Meticulously documenting and extensively researching 191

  The practical steps to achieve success one by one: 193

  Chapter Summary 213

Book one

Introduction

Have you ever considered the power of words? It's astonishing to think that the world around us is constructed through language. From love to war, everything begins with the words we use. Imagine if, like other animals, we had no capacity for speech or if our vocabulary was severely limited—conflicts and wars might cease to exist. Have you ever pondered that many of our problems are rooted in our words? When we argue with a spouse, it's not just a clash of opinions but our language. Disagreements with employers often stem from contentious conversations. Conflicts with children aren't necessarily due to their behaviour but arise from our conflicting words. The values we express and the words we wield can often become weapons in our interactions with others.

Consider wars between nations. They often start because leaders choose the language of pride over understanding. Through language, they institutionalise power, relying on rhetoric, logic, and, eventually, weapons to achieve their aims. Thus, many of our problems can be traced back to our chosen words. Words can shape our lives, leading to either happiness or misery. All human inventions, whether cars, aeroplanes, or computers, began as ideas expressed in words. These mental and imaginative symbols were first articulated in language before being transformed into tangible objects. To successfully navigate life and achieve our goals, we must first examine the words we associate with those goals. We need to adjust and refine them accordingly before taking practical steps forward. This is something I've personally experienced. When I first developed the theory of "psychotherapy words," I wasn't fully aware of their impact on my life. However, after immigrating and having time to reflect, I began to analyse my behaviour and consider my theory more deeply. I realised that the words I had used—both in the past and now—had a profound impact on my mental health and overall well-being.

After years of research and introspection, I understood that many of my problems were rooted in the words I and others around me used. It was a challenging realisation, but it ultimately gave me a clearer understanding of how to harness words to bring about positive change in my life. I concluded that to change my life, I needed to change my words—hence the creation of this book. Throughout its pages, I hope to share my experiences with you and help you see the profound impact that words can have on your life. I also include exercises to help you better understand your situation and ensure you're using the right words.

Words often form in our minds before they reach our tongues and become a conversation. Many of these words are repetitive and emerge in our thoughts without our intention. At times, they linger so persistently that they lead to mental strain. In psychology, this is rumination, which many of us experience daily. Our minds are naturally inclined to unwanted thoughts, which can be harmful when they take the shape of words. Without words, there would be no rumination. As far as science tells us, humans are unique in their speaking ability. Only humans have created thousands of adjectives to describe themselves and others. These traits bring about prejudice, judgment, decision-making, and even wars. Without these words, people wouldn't judge others' actions, and their natural, instinctive behaviour would prevail. Yet, words do not leave us in peace.

When I decided to write this book, I encountered similar ruminations and realised that we must understand the role words play in our lives. Although I had written many books in Farsi, I lacked the confidence to write in English. I didn't grasp the root cause of this hesitation until the voices in my mind brought it to light. There was a voice in my head that stopped me with toxic words, preventing me from writing. I can still recall those words echoing in my mind—words like "inability," "relentlessness," self-conceit, "extravagance," and more. These words formed sentences such as: "How is your book any different from the ones already published? What unique perspective do you offer? Why should you pursue this idea when others have already covered it?"

My mind felt like a besieged, silent city, relentlessly bombarded with these words. Each word fell like molten lava, leaving me defenceless. Exhausted and wounded, I went to bed, wishing to escape those words. "You can't write; you can't write anymore!" they taunted, but they wouldn't leave me. Words enter our minds directly and involuntarily. I don't know what happened that night, but suddenly, the name "Donald Trump" popped into my head. Perhaps it carried a message.

Exploring the Depths of "Dad" and "Father"

When I searched for Donald Trump's name this morning, the first result was his thoughts about his father. Believing in the power of words and their deeper meanings, I was drawn to explore the role of a father in shaping one's goals from the beginning. The words "Dad" or "Father" are lovely, aren't they? They evoke images of a robust and supportive figure—a pillar of strength we can rely on in times of need. In contrast, "Mum" brings boundless love and warmth to mind, much like a comforting embrace. But does "Father" mean support and guidance for everyone? Each word carries its own unique energy, capable of profoundly influencing our emotions. However, the significance of these words differs from person to person. What "Father" or "Dad" means to me may not be the same as what it means to you or someone else. After reading Trump's reflections on his father, who paved the way for his success, I began reflecting on the importance of this word in my life. It is these differences that make our lives unique.

My father holds a special place in my heart, yet I struggle to call him my hero. When I think about his character, I encounter a mix of traits, some endearing and others less so. He was a complex individual, with qualities like intelligence, kindness, and talent, alongside less desirable characteristics such as being demanding, procrastinating, and displaying extreme cynicism towards everyone. This is the first time I've genuinely considered h

is traits in this way, and it's clear that, despite my affection for him, his negative qualities seem to have overshadowed the positive. These traits have become ingrained in my mind.

In his work on "Choice Theory," William Glasser argues that every state and condition a person experiences results from their choices. While I partly agree with this theory, I cannot ignore my father's traits' impact on me before I even understood the concept of choice. Many psychologists believe our personality is primarily formed by age twelve, when we lack the power to make conscious choices. Before we are capable of choosing, we are profoundly shaped by our family and social environment. The harmful words that parents may have spoken, consciously or unconsciously, leave lasting marks on our psyche and influence how we perceive and respond to the world around us.

My father was the first to shape negative thoughts in my mind. He was always cautious, often expressing concern about the intentions of others, fearing they might cause harm. As a result, he protected our family, advising us not to venture too far from home or to socialise too freely with friends. He believed the world was full of potential dangers and wanted to shield us from harm. From a young age, I assumed the world was an insecure place.

When I graduated from university and began job hunting, his advice took on a more practical tone. He discouraged me from dressing appropriately for interviews, convincing me that appearing well-groomed could damage my chances of success. His advice reflected the sentiment of Iran's revolutionary government at the time, favouring the poor over the rich in its slogans. His words emphasised the importance of "power" and "authority," but they left me feeling paralysed, unable to express my abilities. His ideas had become deeply ingrained in my mind and shaped my worldview. Yet, I often wondered about the source of his anxieties and tried, albeit stubbornly, to act against them. What made him so pessimistic and distrustful?

When I entered university, I sought answers to these questions and realised that his family had planted these toxic ideas in his mind. To him, the world was a battlefield where he had to constantly protect himself and his family from potential threats. This attitude stemmed from a lifelong conflict with his stepfather, who had always waged a one-sided war against him. My father's pessimism was a shield that protected him. I began to examine the words my father used and came to believe that he, too, was a victim of the harmful ideas planted in his mind as a child. To understand this better, let me introduce you to my father. If you want to know where your own negative self-talk comes from, consider what your parents used to say.

My father's upbringing in a cold, heartless, and discriminatory family left deep scars on his soul, preventing him from entirely using his intelligence. He was trapped in the cycle of toxic words from his family, and his talents and intelligence were wasted. My father inherited his scars from his family, and I inherited mine from him. Whenever he spoke about his past, I never heard a word of encouragement in his stories. His stepfather constantly belittled him, using terms like "unsalvageable." One day, he took my father to a carpet weaver and asked him to raise his son there. The words my grandfather used reveal the depth of the tragedy: "Don't have mercy on this child; his flesh is yours, but his bones are mine." My father often repeated this sentence. These words, filled with cruelty, lack of empathy, and hostility, eventually became part of my father's personality, shaping his beliefs and thoughts.

My father's childhood was fraught with hardship and sorrow. His biological father, an elderly man with three children from a previous marriage, wed my grandmother after his first wife passed away. Tragically, my grandfather died while my grandmother was pregnant, leaving my father orphaned at birth. As a young widow, my grandmother struggled to raise a newborn on her own. Despite my father's three older half-siblings from his father's first marriage, they never fully accepted him as part of their family. Burdened by poverty, my grandmother eventually remarried, bringing ten more half-siblings into my father's life from her second marriage.

Growing up with ten half-siblings, my father was never embraced as a faithful brother. While it was never explicitly stated, their actions made it clear that he was an outsider. His older half-siblings also treated him with cold indifference. In this environment, my father struggled to find where he truly belonged. The constant sense of exclusion left him feeling isolated within his own family, and despite the hustle and bustle of daily life at home, a deep loneliness overshadowed his childhood. His quest for belonging and understanding became a lifelong battle within his family and the wider world, leading him to believe that the world was inherently unsafe.

My father's first struggle was being labelled as a "step" with his siblings. Although his family treated him kindly, this social label embedded itself in his mind, making him perceive their behaviour as discriminatory. Over time, he internalised these negative words and blamed others for his difficulties. Despite marrying young to escape this toxic environment, he was unable to find happiness and love. He viewed himself as a victim and failed to recognise his strengths and potential. The idea of being a "victim" became so entrenched in his thinking that he saw himself in that light in every situation. As a psychologist, I have observed this tendency in many individuals who struggle with self-doubt and negative self-talk. Tragically, my father never overcame these challenges and passed away without ever genuinely enjoying his life. It is vital, therefore, to be mindful of the words we use to describe ourselves and others. Words can shape our thoughts and beliefs, making it crucial to use them in ways that promote positivity and understanding.

Now, let us consider my father's talents, which he never acknowledged or believed in. When I was a child, my father was an extraordinarily talented carpenter. He crafted all sorts of toys for me and my siblings, including a remarkable car that moved like a real one. In 1975, having such a toy was nothing short of extraordinary. Even as a young child, I could recognise the exceptional quality of my father's craftsmanship. Yet he never seemed to accept my praise. "If I had a sponsor, I could be successful," he often said. I didn't understand what he meant at the time, but as I grew older, I realised he saw himself as a victim. He felt unloved, distant, inadequate, and alone. These feelings prevented him from enjoying his talent or sharing his abilities with others. He refused to accept orders to make toys for anyone else, as if he wanted to stubbornly prove to the world that he was the victim. My family and I loved him profoundly despite his struggles and admired his exceptional work. Yet he persistently downplayed his own greatness, unintentionally rejecting any success that might have alleviated his pain. This habit of viewing himself as a victim kept him from realising his true potential. Nonetheless, despite his flaws, I will never forget my father with deep affection and love.

Here are some more stories that showcase my father's creativity. On one of my visits to his woodworking shop, I noticed a beautiful picture frame hanging on the wall. It was a testament to my father's impressive skills, but what surprised me most was the magic trick he had incorporated into it. The empty frame would suddenly display a picture of my father, and then, with each rotation, the images would change. It was a remarkable innovation for its time. I exclaimed, "Dad, this is wonderful!" But as always, my father responded with the exact words: "If I had support, I could be very successful." I realised he was trapped in these repetitive, disheartening words. For the first time, I saw how deeply this belief was hurting him, causing him more pain with each passing day. As I grew older and built my own life, my father continued to struggle with a crippling lack of self-confidence. These toxic words had controlled his life for years, playing a destructive role within him. Years later, when my father had lost his youthful vigour and was well into old age, I revisited his carpentry shop.

I found him extracting silver from old radios and collecting it in a box. I asked him what he was planning to do with it. The shop was filled with old radios, and he explained that they contained valuable silver and gold that could be mined and sold. Once again, his ingenuity impressed me, and I suggested he could make a good income by recycling these unused items. I tried to show my appreciation and encourage him, emphasising how successful he could be in this venture. But as always, my father's response was the same: "I could be very successful if I had support." For the umpteenth time, it was painfully clear to me that my father was trapped in a limiting belief that had become his identity. Despite my best efforts, I knew it would be difficult, if not impossible, to heal my father's wounds. It breaks my heart to admit that he struggled with a deep-seated belief in his own inadequacy throughout his life. I could see how the poisonous words of his childhood had taken root in his mind, consuming him. Back then, it was uncommon to seek help from a psychologist, and there wasn't even one in town. Those with mental illness were often considered mad. So, it was only natural that my father spent his entire life repeating these ineffective and toxic words, unable to seek professional help. Tragically, with all his talent and ability, my father passed away at the peak of despair, sadness, and pessimism.

Reflecting on my own experiences, I realise how vital having a nurturing and supportive childhood environment is. A simple phrase can sometimes overshadow a lifetime of talent and ingenuity if it's not put into the proper context. Such a phrase can become a mantra, endlessly repeating itself in our minds. Regardless of our potential and abilities, if we fall into the trap of negative beliefs, they can undermine our confidence and prevent us from unlocking our true capabilities. My father's negative "mantras" eroded his confidence, limiting his talents and trapping him in a cycle of self-doubt. I recognise that my father's lack of confidence wasn't merely a personal trait; it had a ripple effect on our entire family. I've worked with clients who have faced similar challenges, and it's often apparent that their struggles are deeply intertwined with their parent's mental health issues. Parental trauma was a recurring theme in many of their stories. This led me to delve into numerous studies and research supporting that our emotions and mental states can be passed on to our children and families. Even more intriguing is the notion that our emotional wounds can affect our close friends, too. Consequently, if one of us is trapped, we can also entangle others.

    I inherited my father's fears and negative words, which fuelled my own hesitation in writing a book. While it's important to be self-reflective, asking inhibiting questions like, "Who will read my book?" or "What value does my writing have?" can be disheartening. The brain often tries to prevent us from pursuing our goals by using the logic of questioning. When I realised that my doubts and negative thoughts were temptations inherited from my father, I also grasped how difficult they are to overcome. It's a complex cycle to break, but I'm committed to rewriting the narrative and showing kindness to myself. My book aims to help people identify their negative mantras and mental patterns and transform them into positive, effective ones that can be used to heal emotional wounds. This mission is essential because addressing and correcting negative mantras can improve our lives and positively impact those around us. I understand how challenging it can be to overcome deeply rooted negative mantras and painful experiences, and I empathise with anyone going through such struggles. However, I also feel proud of those who have already begun their journey towards change. I will guide you in overcoming these obstacles and leading a fulfilling life.

I deeply regret not knowing how to help my father while he was alive. Looking back, I now understand that a few counselling sessions could have made a significant difference in his life. He never saw himself as successful, though I always regarded his achievements as extraordinary. Success isn't solely about grand accomplishments; if we fail to value small victories, even the most significant ones can lose meaning. I wish my father had recognised his own successes and talents rather than constantly feeling like a victim. It's heartbreaking that he endured so much pain and ultimately succumbed to it, never addressing his negative thoughts. Yet, in many ways, he was undeniably a successful person. To fully grasp the true meaning of success, it's crucial to reflect on the concept more deeply. Dwelling on the past can foster negativity, so we must focus on what truly matters. Since I've mentioned "success," let's delve into how it is imprinted in our minds.

We can interpret anything. If instead of Trump, another word—such as "tree"—had occupied my mind, I could have interpreted that too. However, the first thought that came to me that night was Trump, and now I understand why. Each of us lives a unique life, and Trump is no exception. He grew up in a particular family shaped by the values and words instilled in him. I'm not suggesting that the words he absorbed were any better than those my parents instilled in me, but instead, I want to emphasise the profound impact those words had on him. Reflecting on my own moments of hesitation and giving up, I can trace them back to fears passed down from my father.

Similarly, if Trump rises after every failure with renewed confidence, the root likely lies in the words and attitudes his family, friends, or community planted in his mind. I used him as a case study because we all know him, making it easier to compare ourselves. I hope this comparison proves helpful, and in the following pages, I will explore this concept further.

What is success?

It is essential to ask ourselves, "What is success?" We often hear this word come up in conversations. We even see many people beat themselves up because they are unsuccessful. Even a large percentage of depressed people attribute their depression to their lack of success. In our daily conversations, someone often says: "I am not successful in my work compared to other friends." During her heartache, a woman tells her friend she has not had a successful life. A politician might say, "I am not as popular as my friend who is a popular politician." Or a businessman attributes this lack of success to himself compared to other businessmen. Or you may hear a mother say, "My child is not a successful student."

As you can see, this word is often mentioned in comparison to others, and sometimes, it is used as a poisonous word that destroys people's self-esteem and self-confidence. When we talk to these people and ask them why they feel successful or not prosperous, we realise that they are using the wrong word. They judge themselves by comparing their achievements to those of others.

To organise our lives, we must understand and use the depth of words correctly. For example, here are some differences between success and achievement: Achievement is getting everything we intend to get. For instance, we want to get our diploma and achieve it. We want to become an employee somewhere, and we manage to get hired. We have a plan to travel, and we are going to do it. All these are achievements. Success usually refers to achieving goals, achieving desired results, and progressing. When we have a plan and implement it, we turn it into an achievement. The process of reaching the goal, i.e. the result of achievement, is called success. Success is valuing our achievements. Usually, achievement results from an internal need, but more success is the result of an imposed need imposed on us from the outside.

For example, when we are tired of work, we go on a trip, and going on a joyful journey fulfils our inner need, but comparing that our friend travelled to a better country and I could not is an external imposition, and calling it our lack of success in travelling is a mistake. That's why we feel cheerful and happy with every achievement; we postpone our sense of satisfaction until we fulfil imposed needs. For example, after returning from a trip, we feel tired because we don't feel valued or satisfied. We compare the planning process to the execution of the journey with another life and call our success a failure with the wrong word. With this explanation, we should understand that any achievement is a success if not compared to others. The formula for success should be this:

Success begins in the mind before it becomes a reality in our lives. Rather than blindly adhering to the conventional notion of success, which often judges and categorises people, we ought to define success on our own terms and in line with our circumstances. Success is subjective, grounded in personal values rather than being a measurable concept. Instead of comparing ourselves to others, we should focus on our own accomplishments, celebrating each step forward. We can motivate ourselves to strive harder and reach even greater goals by measuring progress. Focusing on "achievement," a concrete outcome of dedicated effort, is far more beneficial than "success," which often relies on external validation. Recognising and appreciating small wins can motivate you to achieve more significant milestones.

Take my father's story as an example. Although he might not have been deemed successful by traditional standards, he accomplished something more meaningful. He was an innovator, creating remarkable things throughout his life. Had he taken the time to appreciate these achievements, he would have felt more fulfilled and enjoyed his life to a greater extent. Unfortunately, he consistently compared himself to his wealthier siblings, attributing his perceived lack of success to feelings of rejection and unworthiness. This mindset followed him throughout his life, preventing him from recognising the value of his own accomplishments. It is essential to acknowledge our achievements and practise self-compassion along the way, as negative thoughts can long-term affect our health and happiness. By caring for our minds and being mindful of what we allow, we can foster a growth mindset, redefining success as an ongoing, empowering journey.

Cognitive Impairment Due to External Factors

Toxic words can result in cognitive errors that prevent us from gaining accurate knowledge. Cognitive errors or cognitive distortions are patterns of thought that stem from negative biases and are not based on reality. These patterns may arise from irrational beliefs or thoughts that we unconsciously reinforce or from biased views of ourselves and the world around us. Cognitive distortions can have a severe impact on our mental health, causing problems such as anxiety, depression, low self-esteem, and low motivation. Although cognitive errors originate in our thoughts, they can have real-world consequences that can make us depressed, anxious, angry, or even suicidal.

To understand cognitive distortions, it is essential to realise how our past beliefs or experiences can influence our perception of something. External factors can also affect how we see things. For example, the Iranian proverb "A bitten snake is afraid of a black and white string!" highlights cognitive distortions. A bitten person may fear anything resembling a snake, even a string.

Aaron Beck, an American psychiatrist, found that many of his patients dealing with depression were operating on distorted thinking and false assumptions. He linked his patients' symptoms to these distorted thought patterns and hypothesised that by changing their thinking, their symptoms would improve. This led to the development of cognitive behavioural therapy, or CBT.

David Burns was another expert who extensively researched cognitive distortions and suggested various ways to correct these thoughts. Both of these psychologists insisted on the need to change dysfunctional thoughts for treatment. However, I believe that cognitive distortions occur before thoughts in words. In fact, words are distorted in our minds first, and little by little, they turn into ineffective thoughts. For example, success can be a positive word, but if used in a perfectionist family, it can gradually take on a negative meaning, and its continuous use can lead to ineffective thoughts.

To better understand the impact of words, here are some common examples of cognitive distortions: polarised thinking, mind reading, mental filtering, ignoring positive arguments, labelling, overgeneralisation, catastrophising, and personalisation. For instance, when you engage in all-or-nothing thinking, you have polarised thinking. In this state, you see everything in black or white, and nothing is grey for you. You might divide the people in your life into two categories: angels and demons. As a result, you may lose a lot of your friends. Similarly, a person suffering from polarised thinking and cognitive distortions may place someone in a group of evil people with the slightest mistake they observe.

In my father's story, he suffers from several cognitive distortions, including polarisation, mental filtering, overgeneralisation, and catastrophising. Although his brothers and sisters were kind, he believed they did not love him and only pretended to love him. As you can see, cognitive errors and distortions can be a prison that is even scarier than the real prison. But when we come back because of these distortions, the first seeds of this crop are words. For example, my father separated himself from his brothers and sisters with the word "stepbrother" all his life. He had heard this word for the first time from his stepfather. Because his stepfather's behaviour was based on discrimination, my father thought that he had become polarised and polarised thinking since childhood. This word made him understand that there are two groups: insiders and non-insiders. The insider group is good, and the outsider group is terrible. Later, he had generalised this bipolar thinking to everything, and these ineffective thoughts had also made his behaviour ineffective, changing his life. As you can see, the root of ineffective thoughts was just one word planted in his mind.

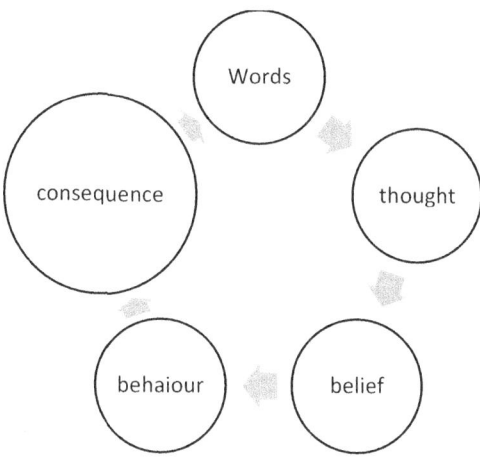

The figure above clearly shows that the word is the first step in our interaction with the world and other people. And words shape our knowledge. Analysing words shapes our beliefs and knowledge, and ultimately, our behaviour is adjusted based on words and beliefs. Our behaviour leads to new events that we call success or failure. Therefore, it is essential to understand the words accurately. We must become familiar with the distorted words that have become known as biased or distorted cognition and be able to re-mean them. So, in the first place, we must understand what role words have had in our lives, and in the second step, we should change our understanding of words and, accordingly, the world. If we face many problems in our lives and want to make a change to live a happier life, we should summarise those problems in words. For example, if I am unhappy in my marriage, I must first define the word marriage for myself. In different families and cultures, marriage has multiple meanings. I must first see which meaning I have attached to this word. For example, in my culture, marriage means the role of housekeeping, cooking and cleaning the house for women and the role of working outside the home for men. If we don't meet this definition of marriage, we will feel like a failure. For example, if our wife is not interested in housework, she has unintentionally come out of our desired world, and we will feel miserable. So, what is the solution? The solution is to think more about the word marriage. Let's see this word from different angles. Let's examine the meaning of marriage in other cultures and see which definition is closest to our lives and can guarantee happiness for us. We must know that our definition of marriage is not definitive but rather a definition imposed on us by the culture and customs of society. By changing this definition, we can get a better result. In fact, to solve this problem, we must first redefine the word, and then our understanding of marriage will change. By changing our knowledge of beliefs, our behaviour will change, and we will be satisfied with life. Although this process seems simple, many of us are so biased to the definitions of words that we cannot change them. So, to avoid cognitive distortion, we must review and reanalyse the words.

I will give another example to help you understand the issue better. For example, someone who suffers from the cognitive distortion of labelling has lived in a family and a society that has always been judged. These people should reconsider the most straightforward words. For example, they have to define the meaning of good or bad for the umpteenth time. If he examines the meaning of the words good and evil, he will realise that these words are rooted in the labels that society and family have imposed on him. For example, the family gives a negative label to their child as soon as he does something wrong. For instance, if a child does not get a good grade in school, they call him "incompetent". This label encourages the child to judge himself and others, and as soon as he gets a little older, they judge people with labels such as worthless, unworthy, and corrupt. In fact, instead of judging others and labelling them, this person judges himself and labels himself. The result of this type of thinking can lead to anger, anxiety, discouragement and low self-confidence.

By using labels, we question a person's entire "character" or "essence" rather than addressing a specific behavioural or intellectual problem. This creates a hostile environment for communication and can even generate hostility between people. One of the significant effects of all cognitive distortions is that instead of correctly analysing and interpreting the words and situations, the person interprets them with a wrong prejudice and submits to his own misunderstanding. This can lead to giving up in most areas of life. I believe the most significant impact of cognitive distortions is giving in to dysfunctional thoughts that affect our entire lives. To explain this better, I will open a new chapter.

The Power of Belief

The power of belief is a fundamental aspect of human life, influencing both mental and physical well-being. In fields like homoeopathy, treatment often relies on harnessing the strength of belief rather than conventional medicine. Patients are frequently treated through their faith in the effectiveness of the treatment, even when placebos are administered. This underscores belief's profound impact on the healing process, as many patients experience noticeable improvements simply because they trust they are receiving genuine medication. The role of belief is not limited to alternative medicine but extends to various conditions, such as COVID-19, where research indicates that belief can significantly enhance treatment efficacy. In some cases, patients given placebos exhibited recovery rates similar to those who received actual medication, highlighting the remarkable influence of belief on the body's ability to heal.

Similarly, the power of belief is evident in psychological conditions like panic attacks. The mere belief that one is experiencing a panic attack can trigger real physical symptoms. Yet, reassurance from medical professionals can alleviate these effects, illustrating the direct connection between belief and physical health. Beyond health, belief shapes our aspirations and goals, often dictating what we think we can achieve. External influences, such as the negative messages instilled in us by others, can convince us of our limitations. This was the case for my father, whose stepfather made him believe in his own inadequacy, a belief he eventually internalised, leading to self-doubt. His story demonstrates how powerful beliefs can be, either propelling us forward or holding us back. It serves as a reminder that cultivating positive beliefs is essential as they shape the course of our lives. True success begins with questioning and redefining these beliefs, remaining open to new insights, and ensuring they are free from bias, ultimately guiding us towards a more fulfilling life.

To surrender or not to surrender

Surrender to what is. Say "yes" to life — and see how life suddenly starts working for you rather than against you." — **Eckhart Tolle**

How we store words in our minds and apply our cultural interpretations to them shapes our lives. Society and those in power often influence us to surrender to specific interpretations of words. For instance, the media and influential figures can manipulate the meanings of words to encourage submission. Take the example of the word "model" - what was once associated with negative connotations has been transformed into a lucrative profession, thanks to a change in interpretation. Similarly, the societal understanding of LGBT individuals has evolved over time due to modern media influence.

Recognising that words hold multiple interpretations is crucial, and our biases can heavily impact our lives. Historically, religious and philosophical figures have used word interpretations to compel submission. Socrates, for instance, manipulated the concept of "justice" through his thought-provoking questions, showcasing the malleability of word meanings. Ultimately, our surrender to these interpretations, whether internal or external, can significantly impact our lives. It's essential to be aware of the power of words and their influence and to ensure that our interpretations are not detrimental to our well-being. We must not unconsciously succumb to words, as they have the potential to dictate the course of our lives.

Although our discussion is about psychology, and we try to show the impact of words in a person's life, avoiding philosophy and religion can also prepare your mind. Most religions, philosophers, and mystics encourage us to surrender. Have you ever wondered what they are asking us to surrender? Yes, they want us to submit to their narrative and interpretation of words. And when we submit to their interpretation, we do what they ask us to do. For example, if we submit to ISIS's version of the word Islam, we can easily behead the opposing people. We first submit to the word Islam, and then we submit to the specific narration and interpretation of that word, and finally, we base our behaviour on that interpreted word.

Deciding whether or not to give up can be a challenging decision. Philosophers continue to debate this complex issue, and some recommend surrender as the best way to find inner peace and unlock creative potential. However, this advice can be misinterpreted and lead to feelings of helplessness and despair. Submission can also be used as a tool by those in power to control and dominate others. It is important to be aware of the different forms of submission and use your own judgment to decide what is best for you.

Blindly accepting everything without taking action can be harmful, and it is important to maintain agency and strive for positive change in life. Before we submit to the interpretation of words, we must first analyse those words many times.

Most religions attribute submission to a total will, often called God. They say that we should submit to God's will, but does the opinion of religions stop here or not? If you look at the religion you follow, you will realise that when you submit to the will of the God of your religion, you must also submit to a particular reading of all other words. For example, if you are a Muslim and submit to God, then you must enter the word hijab into your life and submit to the Islamic interpretation of it. Even your drinking water will be with Islamic interpretation, and unconsciously, you will pass all the words through the filter of Islam and submit to them. With these words, whether you are religious or not, you submit to specific interpretations of words, and this submission shapes your life.

Now, based on the above claim, it is evident that all individuals submit to words, specifically to a particular interpretation of those words, which leads us to discern between positive and negative forms of submission. Understanding this distinction reveals two types of surrender: positive and negative. Positive surrender involves viewing each word we hold biases against through a constructive lens; we first interpret these words by examining them from multiple perspectives, considering their impact on our lives and those around us. If we encounter better definitions, we take those into account, and ultimately, we accept the most appropriate definition and surrender to that word. However, it is crucial to note that this type of submission is not permanent; if we come across more logical interpretations over time, we may reassess our stance. For example, let us examine the word "disabled" using this framework. Initially, we must ask ourselves, what does "disabled" mean? Does it pertain to mental or physical abilities or both? We might conclude that disability encompasses both physical and intellectual limitations. Subsequently, we delve deeper into each category; for instance, what does physical disability imply? We may determine that if we struggle to walk, we cannot move freely, and similarly if we are unable to see or hear, we face significant challenges in communication and perception. Now, we reflect on the implications of these disabilities in our lives. If, for example, this disability pertains to us, we consider its effects: perhaps the inability to walk restricts our mobility, leading to isolation and reliance on government assistance rather than engaging in work. This isolation may prevent us from connecting with friends and the community, ultimately damaging our self-confidence. At this juncture, we must reconsider our interpretation; we might ask ourselves whether others are disabled too. For instance, we could ponder if there are individuals who can walk for hours without fatigue, fly when necessary, or see through walls. The answers to these questions are likely negative, which can reshape our understanding of disability and its impact on our lives.

When the answer is no, your interpretation of the word "disabled" will change, and you will define it as such. No human being has unlimited power, and all of them are incapable of doing many things. However, the degree of this disability is different. By accepting this definition, your view and interpretation of your disability will change. Now, you will submit to this definition, but this submission will not make you weak and captive but will give you the strength to continue with your life.

Positive submission is not submission to incapacity and externally imposed words but to one's own findings. However, these words can always be reinterpreted and changed. Here are some additional features of positive submission:

-Transformation: When you surrender positively, you transform yourself and your life. You change your attitude and behaviours, your habits and routine, your relationships and environment, your reality and destiny, and become a new and improved version of yourself.

- **Agency and action**: When you surrender positively, you do not lose your agency and action. You just use them in a different and better way. You do not give up your power and responsibility. You just practice them in a more effective and meaningful way. You don't stop planning and taking steps. You just ensure they are not ineffective words and are aligned with your purpose and vision. Instead of being a puppet or a slave, you become a strong-willed human being who creates words one by one instead of being trapped by words.

- **Meaning and diversity**: When you surrender positively, you do not lose your meaning and diversity. You just find them different and deeper. You do not lose your individuality and originality. You express them in a more harmonious and balanced way. You do not lose your uniqueness and creativity. You use them more productively and usefully. Instead of being isolated and selfish, you become a part of the whole and a contributor to the greater good.

As mentioned earlier, sometimes submission comes from home and society, and the root of this submission goes back to the culture, religion, and ideology people accept. Surrender can have different meanings in different religions. For example, in Christianity, submission means trusting and following Jesus Christ as Lord and Savior. In Islam, submission means submission and obedience to God as your God and Muhammad as his messenger. In Hinduism, surrender means dedicating oneself to a personal deity or a universal principle. In Buddhism, surrender means giving up and detaching from worldly desires and attachments. In Taoism, surrender means harmonising and balancing oneself with the natural order and way of doing things.

As it can be seen from these definitions, each type of submission forms a different behaviour in people, and submitting to the word brings with it other words that we have to submit to successively, and unconsciously, we fall into a cycle where we have lost our authority. This type of submission is a negative submission. It is surrender with no will, interpretation, or decision behind it and is pure surrender. In this type of submission, a person is like a replica or a doll that is in the hands of others, and they play with him. Before being in the position of a free human being, this person is a captive person who has put each and every word with interpretations in his brain, and he has completely lost his power to interpret words and find the path of life.

In positive surrender, it's not about losing; it's about becoming part of a greater power. In the words of

Rumi: "When a drop falls in the ocean, it loses its individuality and becomes the ocean." This kind of surrender can bring strength and enrichment to your life.

Why do I mention the word "surrender" at the beginning of the book? The reason is apparent: we first analyse the words willingly or unwillingly and then act on them. That means, in reality, we submit to the words we have interpreted or do not have the power to interpret and imitate them. For example, a radical soldier who simply follows the orders of his commander cuts off the heads of others, or a religious person attaches a bomb to himself and explodes himself among ordinary people in order to harm them and believe that he will go to heaven. He has never analysed the word heaven. He just imitated the words of his religious leaders like a monkey. If this person had analysed the word "martyrdom" before taking the first action, he would have realized that he does not become a martyr by killing himself. To reach the concept of martyrdom, this person reads many books, listens to different people's opinions and finally reaches a conclusion. If a person tries to learn without prejudice, he will get a good result and define the word best.

The above example shows that most of the time, we don't analyse words but imitate them. Politicians, powerful businessmen, rich people, religions, and the media use this characteristic of humans to deprive them of the power of thinking and force them to imitate. Therefore, words show themselves to people in the way that the powerful above want.

Even though people can think about words, they are not immune to mistakes. People can understand words through "cognition," but cognition has many facets, and sometimes it can be faulty, affecting a person's conclusions. **Arne Beck** first raised the issue of cognitive distortions, suggesting that our cognition takes a winding path, leading to cognitive contamination. To illustrate this problem, think of knowledge as a river that meanders through different paths and is polluted by various flows, such as sewage and household waste. This river remains polluted if it is not constantly replenished by rain and flowing water. Similarly, cognition constantly encounters polluting factors along its path. In psychology, cognition refers to the act or process of acquiring knowledge and concepts through thinking, experience, and the senses. This concept begins from birth and helps us understand and communicate the meanings of the surrounding world. Cognition serves as the connection between the subconscious and the surrounding world, and it holds various meanings in different fields.

In the field of psychology, cognition encompasses a person's psychological functions, including practical aspects of thought and diverse thought processes. For instance, cognition involves perception, attention, knowledge formation, memory, judgment, intellect, calculations, problem-solving, decision-making, logic, and language production. Each of these aspects, such as perception, attention, and memory, varies from one person to another. This means that our tools for analysing our words can be ineffective.

In order to properly understand our cognitive errors, let's examine some cognitive factors. One of the most important factors of cognition is perception. What is perception, and how do we perceive it?

Perception generally refers to the process of being aware or understanding something through the senses. This can include seeing, hearing, touching, tasting, or smelling, as well as cognitively interpreting these sensory inputs to make sense of the world around us. Perception is fundamental to human cognition and allows people to interpret and interact with their environment.

Now, to make the discussion clearer, consider your upbringing environment. Is the perception of a person who was born in a European and free family the same as a person who was born in a remote, religious, and poor village? Of course not. A person who was born in a religious village has always heard the sound of lamenting and crying for the martyrdom of his imams, has seen his mother and father wearing black clothes in mourning for an unknown person, and even sacrificed himself for that person. The five senses of this person were constantly connected with abstract religious concepts. He has never seen or touched the beautiful body of a girl like a European. He didn't listen to happy music or great works of music like **Beethoven** and **Bach**. Under these conditions, is this person's understanding of the world equal to that of another? Of course not. So, different understandings can affect our knowledge. If you were asked which of the above two groups is more prone to tie a bomb to themselves and blow themselves up among other people, what would your answer be?

The differences in how humans see, hear, and speak are due to their different understanding. These different understandings can lead to errors in word analysis. For example, two groups may have quite different analyses of the word "woman". One group may see a woman as a prisoner and not allow her to do anything without a man's permission, while the other group may see her as a free individual and not interfere in her life. These different analyses, resulting from our cognition, can significantly impact our entire lives. If we examine the thoughts in our minds, we will gradually understand how word analysis can affect our lives.

It's evident from the above topic that different cultures and societies provide different understandings. We are not trying to criticise them here, but a fair examination reveals that some societies tend to nurture unsuccessful, unhappy, angry, fanatical, persuasive, and rebellious individuals. All of this is due to the misconceptions of words that arise from misunderstandings. If you feel unsuccessful, it may be because you have defined success based on your cultural concept. If you look at it more broadly, you may realise that you are a very successful person or at least inclined towards success.

Let's discuss the perceptual errors that lead to cognitive errors. Perceptual errors are identified through perception and can occur in various areas:

> **1. Sensory perception:** This refers to errors in how the brain interprets sensory information. For example, optical illusions can lead to visual perception errors, where what is seen does not correspond to reality. A mirage, for instance, may appear to be a body of water, but as we approach it, we realise that it is not real. Religious groups sometimes may exploit sensory perception errors by claiming to represent a divine entity. They may induce sensory perception errors by suggesting that

the form of a spiritual figure is visible. This can lead people to become superstitious and believe in supposed miracles performed by individuals who exploit these errors.

2. Environmental and Family Education: The training we get from the environment and the family during our lives forms our understanding. These tutorials affect our taste, passion, desire, and even pain. For example, a person born into an Indian family and raised because of the steep eating of foods has no sense of pepper eating, while people in other cultures will have an unpleasant and painful sense of pepper. The mythic **Mircea Eliade** shows how some primitive tribes are in the face of pain and do not even feel it. For example, in some tribes with a unique aesthetic, the large tribe with a knife takes the body. This is more about women who want to look more beautiful; for example, their face creates different grooves with knives that look more beautiful. They sit down without protest and give themselves to a sharp knife. These people understand the pain differently from a person who lived in a European or progressive society and has seen his parents' fear with the slightest wound. This person feels pain with the slightest injury. So, knowing these two groups for environmental and family education is essential in most cases.

3. Perception of the bias: Many factors can influence our perception of concepts, news, behaviours, and even events. For example, if someone is involved in an accident and is severely injured, their understanding of the event can vary based on their religious beliefs. A religious person may attribute the accident to a higher power, interpreting it as a divine test of patience or as a message from God. Meanwhile, a non-religious person may analyse the incident more practically, focusing on factors such as driver error or individual mistakes. As a result, the perceptions of these two groups can be quite different.

The influence of bias is not limited to the aforementioned category; there are thousands of other factors that can contribute to it. Technology, for instance, can be a significant source of pervasive bias. Individuals are inundated with numerous pieces of fake news on a daily basis, and due to their reliance on what they hear and see, they often perceive these stories as real, shaping their understanding. This bias plays a significant role in politics. For example, when political opponents of a public figure disseminate news or videos online, it leads to widespread discussions about the content. Even if the news is later proven to be false, its initial impact on people's perceptions remains. In particular, those who oppose the individual in question continuously propagate negative news, thereby influencing people's perceptions. To elucidate this topic, we will examine the case of Trump to illustrate how our perceptions can be influenced.

I have only assumed the above four cases so that you can become aware of the complexities of the subject and know that even if you want to analyse words carefully, many factors can change your understanding of words. But don't worry, despite all these obstacles, there are many ways that you will be able to escape the trap of misconduct and biased cognitions and get more accurate knowledge. Throughout the book, I will refer to precise word analysis methods so that you can successfully become familiar with the words and act on them.

Stop reading

Have you ever encountered people who read countless books but can't hold a ten-minute conversation about them? Or perhaps you've experienced the frustration of thoroughly enjoying a book, only to forget its contents almost immediately after turning the last page? It's a situation we've all found ourselves in. But why does this happen? The truth is that our brains are wired to forget because they are bombarded with thousands of topics each day. In order to protect themselves from overload, they discard much of the information we encounter. This is why simply reading a book doesn't have a lasting impact on our views or behaviours. The key lies in practice – continuously revisiting and reflecting on the most essential points to fully internalise the book's teachings.

In reality, reading is only the first step in the journey of acquiring knowledge. If we don't apply what we learn, it fades quickly from memory, making the entire exercise seem pointless. This is why novels often leave a stronger imprint than academic books. When we immerse ourselves in a story, we revisit it, empathise with its characters, and mentally replay the events, keeping the narrative alive in our minds. In contrast, theoretical or academic texts can easily slip away unless we actively engage with the material. To counter this, I propose a simple but effective strategy: assignments. When you reach key sections of a book, pause and reflect. Summarise the text and discuss it with friends, family, or colleagues, challenging the ideas along the way. These discussions solidify your understanding and ensure the book's lessons stay with you. If there's no one to chat with, speak to yourself in the mirror or jot down notes. This approach deepens your grasp of the material, transforming reading into a truly enriching experience.

Summary

- Power of Words:

- Words are the foundation of our world, influencing everything from love to conflict.

- Our problems often stem from language, affecting relationships and societal dynamics.

- Changing one's life involves changing the words used, leading to positive transformation.

- Exploring Toxic Words:

- Certain words like "unable," "unworthy," and "cowardly" can shape our thoughts and lives negatively.

- Toxic words can originate from upbringing and societal influences.

- Understanding and healing emotional wounds involves identifying and altering the impact of these words.

- Understanding Success and Achievement:

- Distinguishing between success and achievement: Success is about achieving desired results and progressing in life, while achievement is reaching specific goals.

- Success involves valuing achievements and can be influenced by internal and external factors.

- Cognitive Impairment Due to External Factors:

- Toxic words contribute to cognitive distortions, impacting mental health.

- Cognitive distortions can lead to anxiety, depression, and low self-esteem.

- Understanding cognitive errors and distortions requires analysing perceptions, environmental influences, and biases.

- Positive vs. Negative Surrender:

- Positive surrender involves interpreting and understanding words to make informed decisions.

- Negative surrender entails blindly accepting interpretations without critical analysis, leading to loss of agency.

- Various religions and ideologies promote different surrender forms, shaping individuals' behaviours and beliefs.

- Perceptual Errors and Cognitive Distortions:

- Perceptual errors can arise from sensory perception, environmental influences, family education, and biases.

- Factors like religious beliefs can influence how events are perceived and interpreted.

- Despite challenges, methods for accurate word analysis can help overcome cognitive distortions and biased cognitions.

Activity

Among the thousands of influential words, I pay more attention to the word "submission". Understanding other words ultimately leads to their acceptance and submission to those words. In your first exercise, you need to review the word "submission" and write a list of behaviours, decisions, actions, beliefs, and situations to which you have submitted. Discovering the true nature of surrender can be a powerful tool for positive change in one's life. You should be able to analyse which type of submission was due to disability, coercion, ignorance, or neglect and which submission was voluntary.

By exploring various forms of surrender and understanding their potential benefits and dangers, we can make informed decisions about our lives and take meaningful steps towards the future. Whether through the evolution of our attitudes or through a more harmonious being, it's important to understand that every action we take is based on surrender, whether or not it is desired.

For example, when you are expelled from a company, your perception and understanding of the word "expulsion" will influence your emotions and behaviour. If your perception and understanding of expulsion is negative, you may exhibit impulsive and nervous behaviour. However, if your perception is positive, you may calm down and focus on finding a better situation.

It's important to differentiate between positive and negative forms of surrender. By doing so, we can harness the power and enrichment that comes from positive surrender and avoid blindly accepting negative surrender as the only solution.

I ask you to be honest with your feelings and thoughts in this section. Remember, you have the power to reflect on your past experiences and identify the areas where you may have missed the mark. Identifying the factors that have caused you to surrender may be difficult, but please know that you are not alone. Evaluating where you may have surrendered in your current lifestyle is important, but it's okay if you haven't done so yet. Take some time to think about your experiences and consider everything that may help you create a better future. Remember, you deserve love, care, and compassion, especially from yourself. Write your understanding of the word "submission" on paper and express the perceptions and knowledge that have led to your surrender. After this, you will be able to change your life.

Now you are a new person. You understand the concept of surrender, the influences of perceptions and cognitions on your analysis of the word "submission", where you were mistakenly subjected, and the elements that have led you to surrender.

My definition of "surrender" before reading the book

What do I mean by "surrender"?	
What cognitive factors have influenced its definition	

Which submissions am I unhappy with?	
Which submissions am I happy with?	
How can I have a new definition?	
Which perceptual and cognitive factors should I change?	
How are these changes possible?	
What results do I want to achieve?	

My definition of "surrender" after reading the book

After revising your definitions	
What do I mean by "surrender"?	
Which cognitive and perceptual factors did I change?	
How does the new definition affect my life?	

This assignment is for you to reflect on the word "surrender". After that, you should consider each and every aspect of your life that you have surrendered to. This list can vary for each person and may include things like marriage, work, education, failure, success, war, peace, family, illness, health, affection, love, hate, rejection, happiness, and sadness.

The trap of doubt

The Eagle with a Broken Wing

Once upon a time, a majestic eagle soared in the sky. This eagle had strong wings and sharp eyes to detect prey. It was circling the vast expanse of water, looking for the perfect target to land on. However, something disturbed this magnificent bird. Doubt filled his mind as the eagle contemplated his next move. What if the bait was too heavy? What if he can't carry it? These conflicting thoughts created a cloud of confusion and overshadowed the eagle's usual confidence. Despite his powerful wings and the freedom to roam the sky, the eagle felt grounded by uncertainty and despair.

In fact, the eagle's wings were physically healthy, but its mental wings were broken. It flew aimlessly, unsure of which prey to pursue. Confused and disheartened, he turned around in the sky, but finally, he could not catch good prey and returned to his nest. Hunger prevented him from sleeping. He could hear other eagles joking and laughing with their families. He slept in his nest with sadness and hunger, and when hunger forced him more, he came out of the nest slowly, tired and disappointed, but he was unable to fly. He looked around and saw the rest of the food the other eagles had thrown out. He slowly went to the remaining carcass of the rabbit, brought it to his nest, and began to eat it eagerly so that they would stay alive!

Do you believe this story? Of course, you don't. I'm not trying to tell you a fictional story; I want to draw your attention to one issue. Why is this story unbelievable? There are several reasons, but I will mention only a few.

First, the eagle does not work by reason but instinct, and when the hunger instinct commands it, it rushes towards the first available prey.

Second, what the eagle learns is instinctive; for example, if it rushes towards a dangerous animal once and gets hurt, it will not go towards it again. Because he instinctively understands that going in that direction is dangerous.

Thirdly, the eagle does not give multiple meanings to words like humans. Every word has a meaning for him. For him, hunting is a means to eat and survive. He does not value that burden, nor is he blamed for hunting, nor is he proud and applauded. Therefore, hunting is only hunting. Therefore, no depressed and sad eagle returns to its nest without hunting and does not feed on other people's extra food. So, if helplessness is possible for an eagle that does not have reason and intelligence, why do we, who have reason and intelligence, become helpless? As I mentioned earlier, the reason for our helplessness is reason, or rather, it is due to the wrong use of reason.

Everyone lives somehow. We can live like a wounded eagle with broken intellectual and emotional wings, but this life will not give us more. If we don't change the words and want to value them as an obstacle in our lives, we will get the only food left from other people's lives. In this case, dreams and sky-high goals seem out of reach. To truly achieve what we want, we must heal our wounds and regain our ability to fly. A broken eagle's wing represents obstacles in our minds and negative beliefs that hold us back. We can spread our wings again and soar towards our dreams by healing these wounds.

Toxic Beliefs

Our beliefs can be influenced by various sources such as education, religion, tradition, friends, authority figures like governments and capitalists, or the media. If we unquestioningly adopt these beliefs, they can become deeply ingrained in us, potentially leading us astray if they are incorrect.

One-way toxic beliefs can take root is through the influence of others. For instance, surrounding ourselves with constantly negative and critical people can sow seeds of doubt in our minds, making it challenging to pursue our goals.

Let me tell you about a client whom I'll call Claire. Initially, she seemed kind and pleasant, but she struggled with attending sessions due to financial concerns. Surprisingly, I discovered that she earned more than double the average salary. It became clear that Claire had substantial savings but was hesitant to spend any of it. After some discussion, I was able to convince her to attend another session, during which we focused on her relationship with money. It turned out that Claire lacked a clear understanding of concepts like "money," "poverty," and "wealth." For instance, she expressed uncertainty about what money truly meant.

I had to challenge her to provide a better definition of money subtly. That's why I mentioned the word poverty; she defined it as not having money. To clarify our discussion, I asked her about Gandhi. I asked if Gandhi, who had no money, was considered poor. She quickly responded that Gandhi was not poor. When I asked how Gandhi was not poor and if poverty meant not having money, she couldn't answer. We continued our discussion, and I asked about her family to understand how he developed her negative beliefs about money. She mentioned her father's conservative views on spending money. She explained that her father instilled in her a deep fear of spending her savings, believing that she would lose it all and risk her survival. This fear led her to accumulate wealth in a bank account, influenced by toxic ideas instilled by her father. Her father had convinced her that taking money out of the bank account would be like creating a hole in a dam, causing all the water to rush out.

I used the dam example to explain her fear of spending money. I likened her bank account to a dam holding her money, and she feared that spending any of it would cause a flood. She couldn't refute the analogy. I didn't wait for her response and let her ponder it.

Despite appearing successful to her friends due to her lucrative job, she was troubled internally. Her fears about money prevented her from truly enjoying her financial resources and hindered her overall well-being. Unfortunately, such harmful behaviour is common among many parents. Some use fear tactics, while others undermine their children's self-esteem and confidence. Negative feedback and insinuations of inadequacy or unattractiveness are distressingly common. These actions and statements contribute to toxic beliefs in young minds. To achieve our goals, we must start by clearing our thoughts.

In this client's case, I believed that analysing and redefining keywords related to money and wealth could change her outlook on the world. While this client's beliefs stemmed from her father, others may form their beliefs differently. It's essential to explore each one. Toxic elements can also enter the mind through personal experiences. Trauma or abuse can leave lasting scars on the mind, manifesting as negative thoughts and beliefs about oneself, others, and the world.

When John came to our counselling session, he seemed frustrated and anxious. He expressed his feelings and said, "I'm trying to find my way. Every job I do ends in failure. Even when I tried to change my job, I was disappointed again." When I delved deeper into his thoughts, it became clear that he was not persistent enough to stay in one particular job. He immediately moved on to a different career path whenever he failed, only to find that his past experiences were ineffective in the new role. His history was full of unrelated experiences. His train of thought seemed to mislead him. Instead of reflecting and analysing his failures, he would quickly move on to the next attempt. It was as if he was internalising his failures, which led to a cycle of despair and self-doubt.

John's failures stem from his childhood experiences. If we fail to learn how to deal effectively with problems, we risk getting stuck in repetitive cycles that make it difficult to break free. John did not know how to solve problems, so he went from one predicament to another. To conclude the discussion with John, I emphasised "job" and asked what he meant by the job. He said that a job is a way to earn money. I asked him whether he had any income from all the jobs he tried. He said yes, some of them had a good income, but growing in that job was impossible! I made him understand his definition of the job. I said, but you believe that a job should lead to income, and you had income, so why did you leave it? He said that it was not possible to grow in that job. I said: So you have to change the definition of job. He shook his head. I said that if we accept what you say about the job, we can interpret it like this. A job means earning money and hoping for a job promotion. He smiled in satisfaction. He was happy that my definition of a job confirmed his central belief. Then I asked him about his last job. He said he was an employment consultant. I asked him about the organisational chart of his department. He enumerated each and every related job. I asked him if, if someone performs better in the employment consultant position, he can be promoted to a higher position. His answer was yes. He said that the executive director of their company used to be an employment consultant!

Once toxic elements enter the mental cup, it is difficult to remove them. However, we can do a few things to protect ourselves from their harmful effects. First, we must reduce our problems to one word. For example, if my problem is to change my job, I should focus on the word "job". Second, I have to examine the different aspects of that word from different angles. Third, I must specify the advantages and disadvantages of each point of view. Finally, choose a point of view or a combination of several points of view and accept them as your belief about the job, and finally, take your actions based on the new belief. Finally, if our efforts are insufficient, we can seek professional help. With proper treatment, word change performance can be improved, and the impact of brain damage can be reduced.

Ineffective words produce negative emotions

Our brains have the ability to link words with feelings and behaviour. The way we perceive words influences our emotions and actions. Even simple words that we don't think about can impact our brains. For instance, when the word "lemon" is mentioned, your brain may send signals connected to sourness, causing the cells and glands associated with sourness to react, making your mouth water. Even before you've tasted a lemon, just hearing the word can make your mouth water. This is a basic example, but the impact of words goes beyond this.

For example, the word "father" doesn't have the same effect on everyone as the word "lemon" does. The meaning of this word varies for each person based on their upbringing, the behaviour they observed from their father, and many other factors. This difference in word interpretation triggers different emotions. If your father was strict, angry, unemotional, and critical, hearing or using the word "father" may evoke negative emotions like anger, despair, abandonment, and sadness. Conversely, if your father was supportive, kind, and selfless, using this word may bring about positive emotions such as happiness.

If you experience negative emotions, try to identify the root of these feelings in the words you use. Your emotions will change accordingly once you identify these words, analyse them, and find alternatives.

Words that produce negative emotions can include those we unconsciously use to describe ourselves or our situations. For example, words like "can't," "always," and "never" can lead to negative thought patterns. When you tell yourself, "I can't do this," your brain accepts this as truth and generates feelings and behaviours in line with it. Such words not only reinforce negative emotions but can also reduce motivation and increase anxiety and stress.

The solution is recognising ineffective words and replacing them with more positive and empowering ones. Rather than saying "can't," focus on the word "can". What do you mean by being able to? What are the limits of your ability? How much can you do, and after what point do you struggle? By analysing this word, you will realise that using the word "can't" may be inaccurate. These simple changes in language and vocabulary can have a significant impact on how you feel and act.

The effect of negative words on behaviour

Our brains can be vulnerable to toxicity, preventing us from achieving our goals. Inefficient and negative words not only cause negative feelings in ourselves, such as weakness and indolence, but they can also lead to negative feelings towards others, such as jealousy, aggression, and anger toward people who are successful in our opinion. These negative emotions can harm our well-being and even lead to physical illness. They can also damage our relationships with others.

Some may believe they have coped with their negative feelings and succeeded despite them. It is important to understand that even if you achieve your goals with jealousy, the consequences will be negative. For example, if you become rich with envy, you will not find peace. Instead, you continue to belittle others and use your wealth to make them feel inferior. Your jealousy simply becomes another form of toxicity.

The first step to overcoming addiction is to improve your mental vocabulary. Just like an eagle rejoices in the success of other eagles, you must learn to celebrate the successes of others. This can only happen if you change your mental words, improve your cognitive abilities, and find meaning in your life.

Remember, you are not alone. Everyone experiences negative emotions from time to time. However, you can learn to manage your emotions in a healthy way and achieve your goals.

We need to achieve three main goals: redefining the word success, discovering the paths to success, and taking action to achieve it. This book will take you on a journey that will guide you to success and help you understand its importance. As you flip through the pages, you will experience a sense of satisfaction as you discover your innermost desires and gain a comprehensive understanding of your accomplishments. I use Donald Trump as an example to help understand the model presented in this book. By studying his life, we can learn how to use personal power and apply practical advice to achieve our goals.

Why Trump

I chose to include Trump in my analysis for several reasons. First, Trump was heavily criticised by a large part of society. It is important to consider whether these criticisms were based on our own knowledge or if we simply imitated others. Second, what specific characteristics of Donald Trump did we find distasteful? These features should be reviewed while reading the book. **Debbie Ford** addresses an important issue in the book " **The Dark Side of the Light Chasers** " She suggests that when we are unhappy with someone's character or actions, we must recognise that those traits may also exist within ourselves. We should consider this the "dark half" of our being and strive to reconcile with it rather than accusing others. Third, Donald Trump is widely regarded as a successful figure in the economic field. I will attempt to understand his attitude towards the world to comprehend the reasons behind his success. By reading his words from his perspective, we can gain insight into how he formulated his beliefs and mental processes. It is important to note that this book does not evaluate any accusations against him. Trump, like any other human, is fallible and makes mistakes. However, the book goes beyond examining his faults and serves as a spiritual exercise, offering insights into the paths to success.

Examining Trump's successes in business and politics, regardless of our judgments about his character, can help us learn and grow. Using Trump as a case study, we can overcome negative emotions, find inner peace, recognise and correct ineffective words, and acquire the skills necessary for success.

I wholeheartedly acknowledge that Donald Trump served as the President of the United States for four years. He achieved this position through unwavering ambition, meticulous planning, laser-like focus, and relentless effort. Despite criticism from his opponents, millions of Americans supported him. Therefore, it is important to accept that Trump is neither an angel nor a devil. He is, in fact, an extremely skilled individual with a remarkable ability to recognise opportunities and capitalise on them. True success does not result from luck but requires intelligence, talent, and effort. Rather than focusing on his negative traits, it is much more helpful to remember him as someone who achieved success through personal growth and his own methods.

My approach to personal development is based on self-criticism and logical thinking. By scrutinising my beliefs and evaluating external influences, I can ensure that my thoughts are based on reason. Applying logic to all situations, even with adversaries, allows me to overcome challenges with a constructive and open-minded approach. This continuous self-reflection and critical thinking process enables me to achieve personal and professional growth.

The book is divided into three comprehensive chapters, each examining vital aspects of personal growth. The first chapter, "Power," thoroughly examines the different types of power and the methods of attaining them. It comprehensively explores the topic and offers practical tips and strategies to help readers achieve their goals. The second chapter, "Wanting," focuses on identifying and expressing personal desires and goals. Understanding our aspirations is essential, and this section provides insightful guidance on effectively pursuing them. Finally, the last chapter, "Methods," provides practical approaches to achieving individual aspirations and harnessing personal power. It systematically reviews different methodologies and provides concrete strategies to achieve goals.

Approaching this book with patience and a long-term perspective is crucial. Immersion in the content over time allows us to change our core beliefs and use the suggested techniques to lead us to the desired results. Conscious and intelligent interaction with the material is critical to unlocking success in any endeavour. It is recommended that you strive to become ambitious, just like an eagle that is injured but can regain its strength and heal itself. This book has the potential to transform every reader. Every wound can be healed, and this book accelerates personal growth and empowerment. If you are ready to embrace the power within, I encourage you to begin this enlightening journey.

Activity:

Activities for Readers to Understand the Impact of Words and Beliefs

Activity 1: Understanding Word Associations

Objective: Explore how different words trigger different emotional responses.

Instructions:

1. List Creation: Write down a list of common words that you use daily. Examples include "success," "failure," "family," "friend," etc.

2. Emotional Response: Next to each word, write down the immediate emotion or thought that comes to mind.

3. Reflection: Consider why certain words evoke specific emotions. Consider past experiences, societal influences, or personal beliefs that might be contributing.

4. Discussion: Share your list and reflections with a group or a partner. Discuss how different words can have different meanings and emotional impacts for different people.

Activity 2: Reframing Negative Words

Objective: Identify and transform negative words and beliefs into positive ones.

Instructions:

1. Identify Negative Words: List words or phrases you often use that have a negative connotation, such as "can't," "never," "always fail," etc.

2. Reframe: Write a positive alternative for each negative word or phrase. For example, replace "can't" with "can try" or "always fail" with "can improve."

3. Application: Practice using the positive alternatives in your daily life. Whenever you catch yourself using a negative word, consciously switch to the positive alternative.

4. Journaling: Keep a journal to track your progress and reflect on how changing your words affects your emotions and actions.

Activity 3: Belief Exploration and Redefinition

Objective: Explore deeply held beliefs and redefine them if necessary.

Instructions:

1. Identify a Belief: Choose a belief you feel may limit you. For example, "I am not good enough" or "Success is impossible for me."

2. Analyse the Belief: Write down the origins of this belief. Reflect on where it came from, who influenced it, and why you hold onto it.

3. Research: Look for evidence that contradicts this belief. Read success stories, seek opinions from different thinkers, and gather data.

4. Redefine: Based on your research, redefine your belief more positively and empoweringly. Please write down the new belief and how it changes your perspective.

5. Affirmation: Create a daily affirmation based on your new belief and repeat it daily to reinforce the positive change.

Activity 4: Case Study Analysis - The Eagle with a Broken Wing

Objective: Understand the metaphor and its application to personal growth.

Instructions:

1. Read the Story: Read "The Eagle with a Broken Wing" story carefully.

2. Discussion Questions:

- What does the eagle's broken wing symbolise in real life?

- How does doubt affect the eagle's ability to hunt and survive?

- How can we relate the eagle's experience to our lives and challenges?

3. Personal Reflection: Reflect on a time when you felt like an eagle with a broken wing. What doubts held you back? How did you overcome them, or what could you have done differently?

4. Action: Create a plan to address any current doubts or obstacles in your life. Write down specific steps you will take to "heal your wings" and pursue your goals with confidence.

Activity 5: The Power of Belief - Experiment

Objective: Experience the impact of belief on performance.

Instructions:

1. Select a Simple Task: Choose a simple task you can measure, such as solving a puzzle, running a short distance, or doing a mental arithmetic challenge.

2. Set Belief Conditions: Perform the task twice under two different belief conditions:

- First, convince yourself that you will fail (negative belief).

- Second, convince yourself that you will succeed (positive belief).

3. Measure Performance: Record your performance under each condition. Note the time taken, accuracy, or any other measurable aspect.

4. Compare Results: Compare your performance under the negative and positive belief conditions.

5. Reflection: Reflect on how your belief influenced your performance. Discuss how this experiment can be applied to more significant challenges in your life.

Engaging in these activities can help you better understand how words and beliefs shape your emotions, actions, and overall well-being. It can also help you learn to identify and transform negative influences, leading to a more empowered and fulfilling life.

BOOK TWO

Chapter 1
The power

The most common way people give up their power is by thinking they don't have any.

Alice Walker

Power is not inherent but acquired

In simple words, imagine **Shakespeare**, the old writer guy, saying, "To be or not to be, that is the question." He's not talking about some tricky riddle; he's talking about something big: power. Being means having power. **Nietzsche**, another smart guy, talks about the "will to power," which is basically what keeps life rolling.

In both human and wild animal life, the primary goal is survival. Without the ability to survive, life loses its meaning. Power is necessary for survival but not just about staying alive. To organise our thoughts, we must first understand the word "power," which we will explore in this chapter.

Now, conflicts and disputes often arise because people are dissatisfied with the amount of power they have. Throughout history, humans have fought to gain more power. Sometimes, they used religion as a pretext, and at other times, it was about who was in charge or even gender conflicts. But essentially, all major conflicts occurred because people sought more power and ended up causing harm to one another in pursuit of it. It's a long history of individuals constantly striving for more power without realising the potential power they already possess. When you are unaware of your own worth, how can you strive for more?

Consider my dad's story, for example. He spent his whole life feeling down because he didn't think he was successful. Despite being incredibly creative and intelligent, his concept of success was tied to power. He couldn't come to terms with the power he already had and spent his life trying to acquire more. Rather than discovering his potential power, he neglected it. When someone cries over failing a test or losing their job, it's like crying because they didn't obtain power from their situation, even though everyone possesses a lot of power. Imagine the following: the undesirable thing that often leads to conflicts is the pursuit of more power. On the other hand, the very thing that motivates people to work hard and make a positive change in the world is also power. It's a double-edged sword – it can cause trouble but also drive us to accomplish incredible things. Everything starts with the idea of power.

Consider this example: Some individuals try to keep up with others by purchasing expensive cars, houses, and clothing that may be beyond their means. Why do they do this? Owning these lavish items seems to demonstrate a great deal of power. Subsequently, others strive to emulate this power. It's a cycle!

I have heard multiple times from my clients who have evaluated themselves as less intelligent, less capable, and less able to achieve their goals than others. They believed that successful individuals owe their success to coming from successful or wealthy families, having a supportive and healthy social environment, or possessing superior genes. As they lacked these resources, they deemed themselves destined for failure. In reality, these individuals do not have a precise definition of power. Although family, environment, and genes significantly influence individual success, it does not mean that individuals without these factors cannot succeed. Most people's failures are not due to the absence of a good family, upbringing, or genes but rather due to their interpretation of these factors. A person can grow and become highly successful in a supportive family and social environment, even with strong genes, but can still experience failure due to their core beliefs. Conversely, the opposite holds. Therefore, power lies not solely in our possessions but in our perspective towards them. To unlock the magical doors of success, we must first differentiate between "having" and "being." **Erich Fromm** beautifully distinguishes this difference in his book **"To Have or to Be?"** An individual who understands the value, potential, and power of being does not attach importance to possessions and understands well that they can acquire anything they desire through being. Humans naturally differ, and these differences encompass aspects such as colour, race, physical strength, gender, and even intelligence. However, these differences are not significant enough to entirely dictate their lives. While genes contribute, the environment, family, and education have an equal or greater impact. An individual with a disability can achieve success through the influence of a good education and gaining self-confidence, while an intelligent and talented person can falter in a negative and unhealthy environment. An individual can succeed without having any of the aforementioned factors, such as a wealthy family, a healthy upbringing environment, or superior genes. Therefore, having any of these factors can be considered a necessary condition for success but insufficient. Hundreds of factors intertwine to make an individual successful, and I will address some of these other factors. So, if you belong to those who believe that you were born into a troubled family, raised in a negative environment, and your family has average genes, and you believe that you are not capable of achieving significant success, you should reconsider your beliefs. You can still acquire acquired powers even without possessing any of those factors. However, to attain acquired power, you must strive more than others. You must ensure confidence in every small step and celebrate every small success. Success inherently involves acquiring power, and every individual possesses the fundamental power of "being." As long as you exist, you hold a form of power. We consider someone successful if they have acquired power in various fields. For example, the power of **Van Gogh** lies in his magnificent paintings, **Shakespeare's** power lies in the magic of his words, **Gandhi's** power lies in his spiritual influence on people, and **Elon Musk's** power lies in his creativity and wealth. If we consider each individual successful, it is because they have gained power. Therefore, to succeed, one must become powerful. Sometimes, people want more power, but they don't understand what it is all about. It's like they're trying hard for something, but they're not exactly sure why. Imagine if they realised that things like kindness, compassion, and empathy are also a big part of having power. If everyone understood that, our world could be a much better and more excellent place for everyone.

Every success is an attainment of power. If an individual accumulates wealth, they gain power. If someone seeks knowledge, they acquire power. Even having good interpersonal relationships makes one powerful. Power comes in various forms, and each individual can attain a portion. This is excellent news because it means anyone can acquire power according to their inherent abilities. For example, **Gandhi** was an elderly and poor man who mobilised millions through nonviolent resistance, standing against capitalism and colonisation. He relied solely on the power of individuality and brought about a significant transformation in India. In essence, Gandhi's reliance was more on "being" rather than "having." He understood that the mere act of being can create significant changes. He had discovered power beyond the conventional understanding of power and wealth. An important psychological problem for many individuals, especially in unhealthy societies, is considering power as inherent and believing that if they were not born into a powerful family, they would never be able to acquire power. This belief hinders them from setting goals and striving to achieve them. In reality, these individuals value "having" more than "being" because they lack many worldly talents, which leads them to perceive themselves as losers. Indeed, an individual's power is not necessarily derived from family wealth or genetic makeup but from their existence. The act of existing itself bestows upon each person a realm of inherent capabilities, forming their foundational strengths. The priority lies in "being," not in "having." On the contrary, there are some individuals who, due to their self-centeredness, consider power as inherent, separating themselves from ordinary people and claiming special privileges for themselves in their quest for power. However, **Alfred Lord Tennyson** says, "Self-respect, self-knowledge, self-control; these three alone lead lives to power." Self-respect, self-knowledge, and self-control are achievable through awareness, and we can learn how to acquire them by elevating our knowledge and consciousness. Lack of self-awareness and failure to respect "being" can lead to feelings of low self-esteem in times of defeat and narcissistic arrogance in times of victory, both of which are detrimental to the mental health of individuals and society. For example, narcissistic individuals admire all their behaviours and attribute all factors of success to themselves. They behave in a manner that suggests they possess a different nature and have supernatural powers. They believe that power has been individually bestowed upon them and that others do not possess that power. Consequently, self-cantered individuals do not strive to improve themselves. Their self-esteem is low, but they have high self-confidence. They seek validation from others, arranging their activities to gain attention and admiration. They do not examine their path for growth and pretend to have been the same way since birth. We Iranians have a saying: "It's as if the sky has split open, and he fell from heaven." On the other hand, some individuals have a self-deprecating attitude, considering their existence as purposeless and deprived. They believe that they were born into a poor and deprived family and in an unhealthy and unequal society and that they will never possess any power in their future life. Such individuals consider themselves defeated before taking action or participating in any competition. This pessimistic view is because they do not understand the meaning of "power." As I mentioned, "primary power" is synonymous with "being." Simply by existing, we possess power. A review of successful individuals' lives shows that at least half were born into poor families and grew up in challenging circumstances.

For example, **Oprah Winfrey** was born into a poor family in Mississippi, but these conditions did not hinder her unprecedented success. Interestingly, it is worth noting that due to the lack of resources in her family, Oprah even wore potato sacks! Forbes currently estimates Winfrey's net worth at $3 billion, and she is the only black woman on the list of the 400 wealthiest Americans. Here's some good news for you: power is not exclusive to a privileged few, but it is accessible to anyone who recognises the power within themselves and strives for self-improvement.

When referencing the concept of "Opera wealth," it is important to recognise that true power does not solely reside in material riches. Instead, the essence of genuine power lies in one's sense of self and ability to tap into their inherent potential. Pursuing financial prosperity is possible, but it should not overshadow the fundamental strength that comes from self-awareness and self-belief. I mentioned Opera as an example because she aspires to attain wealth. However, it's crucial to understand that her self-awareness and unwavering self-belief fuel her journey towards wealth and her capabilities. This principle can be exemplified through the life of Mahatma Gandhi, who possessed little material wealth but wielded more influence and power than most due to his profound understanding of his inner strength.

Even physical disabilities do not necessarily hinder individuals from acquiring material wealth. For example, **Ingvar Kamprad**, the owner of the retail chain stores IKEA, struggled with dyslexia. His childhood was marked by such poverty that at the age of six, he had to sell matches on the streets to help his family's economy. Similarly, a disabled person, like any other human being, possesses the primary power of "being" and can acquire acquired powers by relying on it.

The number of successful individuals who have gone from poverty to wealth is so large that if we mention them, a separate book would need to be written. However, self-deprecating individuals who do not consider themselves worthy of any good attributes or supernatural reasons for their success say that luck has been on their side! However, examining the lives of these successful individuals and interviewing them only points to one thing: perseverance, perseverance, and perseverance. They have achieved success only through goal-setting, focused efforts, and persistence in achieving their goals. They were aware of their human power. They knew that every human being (even the disabled) has a power that can lead to great achievements if recognised and relied upon. However, why emphasise perseverance and write it three times? It is because the most intelligent, creative, and determined individuals will fail if they lack perseverance. They persevered to achieve victory.

Although financial and political powers are not inherent, the power of desire and wanting, the power of will and action, are inherent, and all human beings can benefit from their inherent powers. Relying on inherent powers and pursuing a purposeful path makes the journey towards acquiring powers smoother. We can achieve social, financial, and political success through intelligent observation, learning, and applying knowledge. Therefore, possessing the inherent "power" is primary, and all human beings possess it, while other powers are acquired. So, if I ask what the fundamental power every human possesses is, what would you say? Exactly, that is the power of "existence". It's the power of existence itself. The very act of being alive, of having an existence, is the most foundational power that all creation shares. It doesn't discriminate based on the type of existence; it's a universal truth. This notion of existence is essentially "being."

Wrap your mind around this: if you are alive and you exist, you hold inherent power. Of course, when I refer to inherent power, I'm not talking about your family's wealth or the genetic and environmental factors that shaped you. I'm referring to your authentic essence, your actual state of "being," and the fact that you "exist." It doesn't matter if you're dealing with health issues or facing disabilities. The simple fact of existing is, without a doubt, the primary power that remains regardless of any disabilities or mental challenges you might be grappling with. Embrace this concept and keep delving into the contents of this book. There's a remarkable journey ahead as you uncover and appreciate this profound power of existence.

Trump's ascent to substantial financial and political prowess, and consequently, his acquisition of social influence, has not overshadowed his essence of "being." He recognises that his fundamental strength lies in his existence, and his unwavering confidence stems from this fact. Despite hailing from a well-off family background, he draws essential lessons from the sad trajectory of his less fortunate brother's life, realising that power isn't inherently bestowed but earned through deliberate efforts. This newfound insight can potentially revolutionise his self-perception, interactions with others, and perspective on the world at large. Trump distinctly discerns between primary power, which may be bestowed by external factors, and inherent power, which is anchored in one's being. He is openly critical of his deceased brother's actions, with some of these critiques even surfacing in public discussions. This critical examination emanates from a place of profound fraternal affection, stemming from a sense of disappointment that his brother didn't harness his primary power to enrich his existence, thereby leading to a sense of discontentment—an emotion Trump profoundly abhors.

In his autobiography, "**The Art Of The Deal**", Trump candidly reveals how his sibling's life influenced him. Notably, his brother's influence is such that Trump abstains from both alcohol and smoking. Trump highly regards his brother, perceiving him as more intellectually endowed and stylish than himself. The wisdom his brother imparted—urging him to eschew alcohol—left an indelible mark, and Trump regards himself as fortunate to have had this guiding figure in his life.

Addressing the pressing issue of America's opioid crisis in a press conference, Trump's demeanour takes on a markedly sombre tone as he discusses the untimely and tragic demise of his brother, underscoring its far-reaching repercussions on his family. This heartrending episode has left an indelible mark on him, his voice carrying a palpable weight of sorrow and distress. He remarks, his voice laden with emotion, on the gravity of the situation:

"I had a brother, Fred. A great guy, the most handsome man, with the best personality, much better than me, but he had a problem. He had a problem with alcohol. And he used to tell me, 'Don't drink. Don't drink.' He was much older, and I listened to him. And I respected (him)... He also added, 'Don't smoke,' and he said it over and over again. And to this day, I have never had a drink, and I have no interest in it. And to this day, I have never smoked a cigarette.

There are many bad things. He really helped me. I had someone to guide me, and he had a very, very tough life because of alcohol, believe me. Life is very, very, very tough. He was a strong man, but there were tough and difficult conditions... But I learned from the individual..."

As evident from his speech, Donald Trump's insights reflect a profound self-awareness. He comprehends the path to triumph and recognises the pitfalls that can lead to failure. Equally, he identifies the individuals who can play pivotal roles in shaping his life's trajectory. This awareness stems from his understanding that every human possesses innate potential, a truth he believes his brother failed to fully tap into due to missteps that hindered his inherent capabilities from flourishing.

Donald's astute grasp extends to the realm of acquired prowess. He acknowledges that one can cultivate and harness such abilities with dedicated focus, meticulous planning, and concerted effort. His sentiments are tinged with a sense of regret, seeing his brother miss out on these opportunities. Instead, his brother's counsel prioritised fortifying virtues like faith, empathy, and determination—inherent virtues in each individual.

Donald acknowledges the delicate nature of financial, political, and social influence—powers acquired over time but equally susceptible to erosion. He draws inspiration from his brother's counsel, mirroring the latter's disciplined lifestyle devoid of drinking or smoking. This choice is a tribute to his "being," recognising that safeguarding and nurturing the core self is the pivotal initial stride. This embrace of one's existence paves the way for advancing towards the realm of acquired influence.

In summary, Donald Trump's insights unravel a journey of introspection and understanding. His narrative underscores the primacy of acknowledging and respecting one's intrinsic worth—a foundation upon which to build the edifice of acquired power. This philosophy, shaped by personal experience and lessons gleaned from his brother, radiates implications for his own life and anyone seeking to realise their fullest potential.

Although Trump has gained significant financial and political power, leading to social influence, he knows these powers are not inherent and must rely on intrinsic ones to acquire them. He approaches his brother's case not emotionally but rather with a rational mindset, altering his own life by setting him as an example. In fact, his personality resembles the ancient archetype of "**Zeus**." While his brother possesses great physical strength and beauty, addiction causes him to lose his inherent power. Now, the younger brother, despite grieving his loss, strives to strengthen his own intrinsic powers to avoid a similar fate. After strengthening his intrinsic powers, he utilises the family's financial power to acquire wealth and additional powers. With self-confidence, he aims to establish a superior position in the world, much like Zeus. He desires a higher status than others and to rule over them, acting as Zeus does.

The Zeus-like personality values reason and logic over emotions. It approaches everything with logical thinking and examination. The Zeus-like man is wise, dignified, and serious. They perceive themselves as powerful in all domains because their mind and intellect work effectively, unaffected by emotions, feelings, or impulses. They embody willpower, control, perceptiveness, and mastery in all aspects. Powerful leaders, kings, rulers, and presidents possess such personalities. Just as they exercise authority and governance over external domains, they also possess self-control and governance over their own bodies. They have a high level of decision-making power, and once they decide to act, they achieve their goals flawlessly. Their actions require no extra effort or struggle; they are naturally superior. They possess excellent memory, and if we were to ask them questions from years ago, they would answer correctly. However, having a Zeus-like personality is possible for anyone and depends on individual willpower. As you can see, none of Zeus's abilities are external; they are traceable within him and every individual. We all possess these powers and must discover them to become Zeus-like.

Therefore, the first step in achieving worldly desires is accepting two important points. Firstly, everyone possesses intrinsic powers, and secondly, acquirable powers are attainable by relying on their intrinsic powers. I do not intend to examine Trump's life here, as we are all aware that he has gained a significant amount of power. It is sufficient to understand that a lunatic or someone with a mental disorder does not attain the concept of acquired power. Achieving acquired powers first requires the discovery of intrinsic powers, and a mentally ill person cannot discover their intrinsic powers. Such an individual may accomplish things impulsively and experience temporary success, but their success is not sustainable. Now, we must understand how to acquire power and strengthen our Zeus-like personality.

Do not think that becoming "Zeus" is a difficult task. Look at Donald. In this short speech, he shows you the way. Try to internalise his words. When his brother advises him not to drink or smoke, what does he mean? Why should he be deprived of the pleasure of drinking alcohol? There is only one reason: to avoid drinking so that he can focus on his goals and be successful. Therefore, to become powerful, 1) abandon addictive and harmful habits, 2) identify your intrinsic powers such as willpower, analytical power, focus, and perseverance, and 3) boldly determine your goals and design a path to reach them. Do not forget that none of these three require wealth, and we all possess them.

Thus, we conclude that financial, political, and social powers are not freely given to individuals; they must be acquired through effort. However, inherent powers are freely available to beings and humans, and individuals must acquire them within themselves and utilise these intrinsic powers to acquire external powers. Therefore, each of us possesses hundreds of intrinsic powers that we must first recognise to harness them and acquire external powers with their help. So, let's start by understanding ourselves and our intrinsic powers.

Self-power of an ant

If we consider power as the ability to perform a task, humans and many other creatures have inherent power, with a major difference being that humans, despite having physical power, also possess spiritual power, which is much more important than physical power. Therefore, with the understanding of this matter, even the most hopeless and depressed individuals should strive for self-empowerment, as even a disabled person, despite lacking inherent physical power due to organ impairment, possesses inherent spiritual power that can lead to great success. With this understanding, there is no excuse for despair. To understand the subject, first consider the physical power and inherent order of a being to understand the concept of power properly. An ant, although never moving towards acquired power, possesses significant inherent powers. With reliance on these inherent powers, ants have been able to live for centuries, resist the most difficult situations, and continue their existence.

Ants belong to the insect category, lacking wings compared to other insects and living in large colonies. They work together as a group throughout the year, searching for and storing food in the natural environment or their surroundings to use during winter. They can carry 10 to 50 times their own weight on their shoulders! Unlike other creatures on Earth, ants do not have ears, which does not mean ants are deaf. Ants use vibrations to communicate among themselves, emitting vibrations to inform and gather together during specific times such as eating or working. This organ, which can generate vibrations, is located below their knees. They can swim. This does not mean they have the tools for swimming like fish, but they can save themselves when they fall into the water or water-filled pits. They can also float on water for a long time. They possess dozens of other extraordinary abilities that can be understood by reading a specialised book about ants.

My intention in describing only a few abilities of ants was to demonstrate that every living being, even the smallest, possesses inherent abilities and power. Now that we understand this, can we doubt the intrinsic power of humans? Although all ants have the same power, inherent power in humans varies. Each of us humans has different intrinsic powers. This diversity is the secret to human creativity. That is why humans rely on inherent powers and strive to acquire other powers based on their innate abilities. If we, like ants, had limited powers, we might never seek to obtain additional powers. Even disabled individuals have intrinsic powers that can set them apart if understood and recognised. For example, **Stephen Hawking**, often called the second Albert Einstein, was completely paralysed and could hardly move even a finger. However, relying on his inherent power, he became the most influential physicist of the century. He held the **Lucasian** Chair of Mathematics for 30 years. He is known for his cosmology and quantum gravity work, especially regarding black holes. Numerous examples like him can be mentioned. However, my intention in this book is not to focus on these individuals but to familiarise you with your inherent power.

James Allen says, "A man is limited only by the thoughts he chooses." This extraordinary statement shows that, unlike other creatures, humans possess the power of thought. We achieve success not only through the wealth we inherit but also through our thoughts. Thousands of thoughts shape our minds daily; only humans possess this power. Furthermore, only humans can select the best thoughts among thousands. If we make a wrong choice, we limit ourselves and will not achieve success. The magic box called the mind contains all the necessary tools for success and failure, and it is up to us to choose which thoughts to embrace and which path to follow. Therefore, through thinking, we acquire countless powers. These powers can be the power of reasoning, intelligence, deduction, willpower, or other powers. I believe that you face hundreds of thoughts daily, which is a miracle. Only humans can confront hundreds of thoughts daily, but this same miracle can also lead you toward failure. The path to victory lies in power to discern and differentiate between thoughts. We must refine our thoughts and benefit from them. We need to identify our inherent powers, note them, and see how much of this power we have utilised. For example, if you have the power of good speaking, have you been able to use it? Most people utilise only a small percentage of their power. Now, with the knowledge of these powers, we must take steps towards acquiring them. Onward to success!

First, it is essential to interpret the word "power." While I have provided my interpretation above, I encourage you to develop your own understanding of this concept. By achieving a clear and personal interpretation, you will be better equipped to discover your inherent and inner powers. To assist with this, you may find it helpful to fill out the table below.

What are my innate abilities?	What percentage of them have I used in my life?	What Results have been achieved?	How do I use all my inherent powers?	How do I predict the results?	What is the reason for not using my abilities?	How do I remove the obstacles?
1-						
2-						
3-						
4-						
….						

To define "power" correctly, it is essential to understand all of your potential. Do not overlook any of your abilities. Even your smallest ability can make a difference between you and others. For example, if you are highly energetic, consider it as your strength. When others get tired of working, you can continue. When others struggle to concentrate on one task, you can focus on multiple subjects. Therefore, if you are highly energetic, use the opportunities it presents instead of seeking medical treatment or trying to fix it. Or, if you have a sense of humour, utilise this ability to have stronger social relationships. After forming strong social connections, you will gain the power to accomplish great things. Even without limbs, you still exist. You must always remember the difference between "having" and "being." You exist even without the power of hearing and seeing. A Successful individual looks at their existential value instead of their possessions. **Helen Keller** profoundly impacted human societies despite her lack of vision, hearing, and speech. It is astonishing for someone who does not believe in the power of existence and only focuses on possessions to understand how a woman without eyes and ears could establish a connection with the world. However, this great woman accomplished it by relying on belief, faith, and perseverance. She had no means to connect with the external world, but she had faith that allowed her to know the world through the touch of her mentor's hand, listen to music, and fall in love. You can now search for "**Nikki Vujicic**" online and see his success without limbs. They were only committed to one thing: "being." The fact that you exist means you possess power. Therefore, we must first appreciate our existence to discover the treasure within ourselves. After identifying your inherent power, you have identified one of the powerful tools for achieving success. However, you know that identification alone is not enough; the application of power holds special significance. Now, you are armed with a force that can change your life significantly. Keep this table with you every day and, at least for the next few months, contemplate only your inherent powers. If you haven't effectively utilised them so far, find the reasons. After identifying the obstacles, take steps toward resolving them. For example, if you have the power of eloquence but haven't utilised it, determine the reasons for yourself. For instance, the reasons could be shyness in public or social anxiety, which may hinder you from expressing this power. Whatever it may be, write it down on the table and then find a solution to overcome it. If you cannot do it alone, seek help from a counsellor. A good psychologist or counsellor can identify your fears, shame, and anxieties and help you eliminate them to take effective steps. Be confident that by relying on your inherent power, you will gain even greater powers, perhaps the most important of which is financial power. Most people pay more attention to financial and political power without considering their inherent powers and existence. However, as I mentioned, there are various types of power. But first, by relying on our inherent power, we must have the power to continue living on Earth, and in the contemporary world, having financial power is essential for this purpose. Although, for me personally, social or spiritual power holds great importance, I refer to financial power for various reasons. First, let me clarify the concept of financial power. Financial power is not an innate quality; rather, it is acquired through deliberate efforts. Therefore, it is crucial to recognise that achieving financial success may remain elusive without acknowledging and harnessing your innate abilities. While it is worth noting that some individuals may have the advantage of inheriting wealth from their families, I want to focus on those starting from scratch. If you aspire to attain financial success, your initial step should involve thoroughly exploring your inherent strengths and assets. From my professional perspective, it is advisable to use the term "financial empowerment" rather than "financial power." This shift in terminology conveys a more inclusive and positive message and underscores the importance of enabling individuals and communities to take control of their financial well-being. By embracing the concept of financial empowerment, we promote a holistic approach to financial education and independence, ultimately fostering a more resilient and prosperous society. Financial stability plays a pivotal role in today's world, making it increasingly challenging to navigate life without it. Now, let's proceed to the following section to elucidate these factors. Are you ready?

Lions die without eating food!

Having financial stability is necessary

It's important to note that everyone defines things, facts, behaviours, and feelings based on their understanding of the world. You may define power from a different perspective and draw your own conclusion. To help you do this, I will present my arguments and define power. You can then examine and define it from your own point of view. Finally, you can conclude by stating what power means to you and what strengths you may have. I will continue in my own way.

Despite criticisms from many philosophers, without power, there is no existence. Man has power from the moment of conception, and this power grows gradually. For example, a sperm has the power to grow, which leads to the development of a fetus into a child within nine months. This innate power is often overlooked by philosophers who focus on acquired powers. However, acquired powers are frequently not recognised correctly. There are different types of acquired power; financial power is just one. For instance, a philosopher who possesses the power of persuasion can change others' opinions on a subject. A spiritual leader who influences thousands or even millions of people with a message has speaking or spiritual power. Similarly, a person who exhibits kindness and creates empathy in a group possesses the power of management. Likewise, someone who thinks creatively about a subject has the power of creativity. This list could go on, but I'll leave it up to you.

While many people rely on financial strength, I will only mention financial strength on this occasion, as many people worldwide may not be able to understand financial strength or realise other powers to gain financial power. According to **Maslow's** hierarchy of needs, the primary human need is basic necessities such as shelter, food, and essential amenities for survival. In the modern world, all these material needs are fulfilled with money. To lead a decent life, a person must adapt to the progress of society. Considering that the modern world is constantly changing, people must adapt to these changes to avoid depression. In today's world, owning a house, car, capital, and a job are common goals, and acquiring financial power becomes necessary for every person. Without financial power, people may struggle to provide for their basic needs, support their families, or pursue education and travel. Therefore, understanding the methods of acquiring financial power becomes essential.

Unfortunately, in contemporary society, families that prioritize spirituality over material wealth often face various challenges. These individuals may struggle to achieve general well-being, feel excluded from social gatherings, and have difficulty obtaining the normal necessities of life. In addition, many may experience a sense of isolation.

It's important to recognise that prioritising spirituality over materialism is a deeply personal and meaningful choice. However, managing social pressures and the potential consequences of this choice can be daunting. Despite these challenges, many individuals and families who have embraced spirituality have been able to live a decent life without focusing on gaining financial power. These people have realised that material things are not authentic, but they can make life easier. Without solely concentrating on acquiring financial power, they try to acquire it moderately and devote the rest of their energy to fulfilling life and finding purpose in their beliefs.

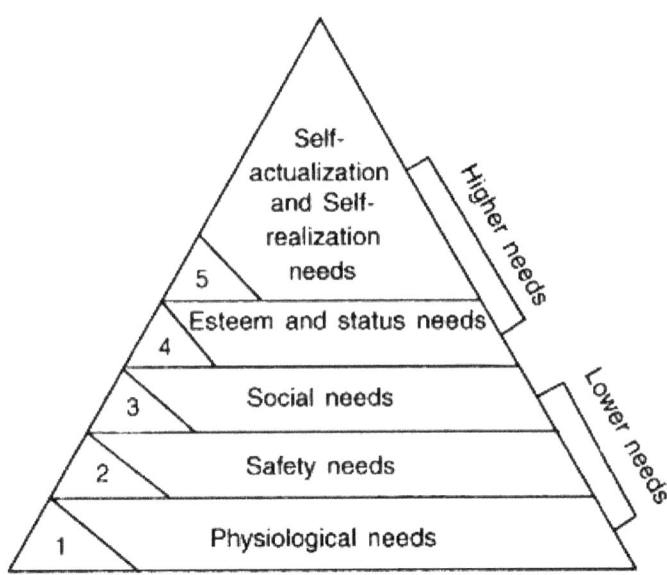

As we have shown, based on Maslow's theory, man will perish without fulfilling his basic needs. So we have to fulfil our basic needs. It means using our inherent abilities and power to take control of our lives. If these needs are unmet, one cannot think about literature, art, self-improvement and friendship. When physiological and physical needs are unmet, a person becomes a prisoner of these basic needs and cannot think about other needs, such as social needs, respect and the need for self-actualisation.

Someone who does not address their basic needs will experience depression, frustration, aimlessness, and, ultimately, premature death. While simplicity has been advocated in various religions and ideologies, it does not mean that wealth is unimportant. Wealth that changes a person's character and turns them into a selfish, oppressive, and unjust being is harmful. Many people lose some of their good qualities after acquiring wealth, leading to the belief that becoming wealthy is equivalent to immortality. For instance, some individuals seek more privileges through wealth, ignore the rights of others, and circumvent the law. These factors have led people to view wealth as a source of immorality and be cautious about it. Therefore, becoming wealthy should be accompanied by personal growth and self-actualisation. If someone puts all their efforts into acquiring wealth but does not grow spiritually, they may become wealthy but burdened by their wealth and used by others instead of living a fulfilling life through their wealth.

Therefore, before considering ways to gain power, you must realise that power can be good. Even if you are spiritual and do not value worldly appearances, you must understand that you need at least some financial power to meet your basic needs. If you wish to remain a spiritual and good person, having financial power is essential to help those in need. However, some religious individuals deny the impact of financial power on people's lives. That is why they constantly collect financial assistance from wealthy people in churches and mosques to help the less fortunate. The problem with religious people is that when they want to preach, they devalue the significance of financial power. They do not talk about how they acquire and construct expensive places of worship. They do not reveal how they make a living without working. Instead, they only condemn wealth and discourage their followers from aspiring for financial power.

From the beginning of human existence to the present day, all injustices have stemmed from the unequal distribution of wealth. There would be no more wars if people could attain financial power equally. Unfortunately, such an opportunity does not currently exist in the world. The policies of communist thinkers have also faced failure. Consequently, we must individually recognise our abilities and acquire financial power through their utilisation. As an "ethically oriented" individual, I seek financial power for the survival and well-being of my family. However, there might be some who misuse this power to demean others. Such individuals will remain weak even with power, as any power contrary to the philosophy of existence becomes self-destructive.

If a politician abuses their political power to harm and torture their people, they are not only powerless but also morally bankrupt. The system of existence will eventually crush such a politician under the weight of justice. Therefore, it is crucial to understand that acquiring power without achieving virtue is impossible. One may become wealthy, but wealth alone does not grant them power. Imagine a wealthy woman who uses her financial power to belittle other women. She is not powerful but resembles a treasurer temporarily responsible for safeguarding the treasury. In contrast, consider someone like Angelina Jolie, who ventures into the most impoverished corners of the world, aiding those in need. She not only converts wealth into power but also enhances the power of others daily. She is not a mere treasure keeper, holding onto her gold and jewels, but rather, she creates power through her wealth, making the world a safer place for others. This power is akin to the power of a divine force.

Many successful individuals recognise the importance of the fact that material possessions do not satisfy their souls; rather, they connect with the human network that gives meaning to their lives. Even Donald Trump understands that being solely dependent on wealth turns him into a narrow-minded person who must devote all efforts to preserving his fortune. This dependence on wealth diminishes his position to that of a mere guard whose duty is to protect his prisoner (the wealth). Hence, he allocates a portion of his wealth to charitable causes. However, there might be some controversy, and some may see it as a deception. Nevertheless, others' opinions do not matter. Even if someone is the purest individual on Earth, there will still be dissenters. Wasn't Christ crucified? Wasn't Socrates forced to drink poison? The crucial point is that individuals must have faith in their chosen path. Although we are still in the initial stage of acquiring financial power, we must understand that accumulating wealth through hoarding turns us into despicable creatures.

For now, we are in the first stage of achieving financial power. It is better to say that we are in the first stage of accumulating wealth, and after acquiring wealth, we will decide how to transform and preserve it as power. This small book will guide you towards the right "thinking" to become rich. Yes, first, our thinking must change. A lion hiding in a cave and being pessimistic about its future, not making any moves, fails to find food, and becomes the prey of vultures. A lion becomes a lion when it moves purposefully, relying on its sharp claws and teeth. Only through willpower, action, and perseverance will it succeed in hunting. Hopefully, you have already come to the conclusion that having the financial power to fulfil a significant portion of our physical needs is essential and necessary. Of course, many of us have experienced numerous failures and have many wounds. But anyone who wants to conquer the mountain peak must endure and even embrace the pain of climbing. Trump's defeat against his rival was a wound, but he stood on his feet again. We must also learn to stand up after falling.

In the first step, I introduced you to your inherent abilities, and you realised how much-untapped potential you possess. Now, after discovering these innate powers, it's time to take the second step, seeking them out. You should hang the following board on the wall of your house and look at it every day.

> *I have consciously decided to attain the power of wealth!*

Know What You Want!

Wanting is not enough; ask and take a step!

In the second chapter, we will delve into the concept of "wanting" and its profound relationship with power. In this chapter, I intend to show that it is crucial to recognise a significant correlation between the two. Merely possessing power is not enough; awareness of the specific type of power you hold becomes instrumental in achieving success. Understanding the various forms of power and discerning where and how to utilise them effectively are essential factors in attaining your goals. To achieve genuine success, we must explore the depths of our desires and aspirations, for these wants often fuel our drive to wield power and influence. Whether we are pursuing personal growth, professional achievements, or making a positive impact on the world, identifying our genuine desires is the first step towards harnessing our inner potential.

The spectrum of power is vast and multifaceted. As I mentioned before, beyond the conventional notions of authority and control, power encompasses an array of attributes, such as emotional intelligence, charisma, creativity, and empathy. Recognising these diverse forms of power allows us to tap into our inherent strengths and capitalise on them to propel us forward.

Moreover, understanding when and where to deploy these powers is equally vital. A strategic approach is necessary, as indiscriminate use of power can lead to unintended consequences. By aligning our desires with our capabilities, we can channel our energies towards endeavours that resonate with our true selves, creating a more fulfilling and purpose-driven path to success.

It may seem easy for you to "desire," but many of my visitors didn't even know what they wanted when they came to me. This pattern of seeking approval from others often leads to constantly pursuing what others have rather than focusing on their genuine aspirations. As a result, their wants and needs may become muddled, overshadowed by the desire to possess what they perceive others to have.

In this journey of self-discovery, it becomes crucial for individuals to take a step back from external comparisons and introspect deeply. By understanding and embracing their own strengths and passions, they can begin to pave their own path towards fulfilment and happiness. So, in the first stage, we need to know what we want. We should be clear about our specific desires and plan the path to achieve them. The process of desire involves certain stages, which I will explain here.

The initial stage of desire involves general aspirations. For instance, a hungry person's general demand is food. When people talk about "desire," they often think of these general demands. However, general demands are more like wishes than targeted desires. Every person inherently demands their basic needs, and without fulfilling them, life becomes difficult. But we must delve into these general demands and specify them precisely to achieve our desires.

Consider someone who desires food. They don't just eat any food; they think about the specifications of the food they consume. If they are a meat-eater, they pay attention to the type of meat they eat. If they are a vegetarian, they research different vegetarian dishes and choose the ones that suit their taste. They also consider their preferences and sensitivities. Are they allergic to certain foods? Do they have conditions like diabetes that require them to avoid specific foods? Moreover, is the desired food accessible in their current situation?

Desiring food, which may seem straightforward, involves many details. Now, imagine when our desires are more significant. If you desire wealth, can you directly move towards wealth, or do you need to specify your desire? The first step towards success and achieving power is to have a general desire. Once you realize that you need something or want to achieve a certain position, you have taken the first step towards success. The second step involves determining the approximate amount of wealth you need. The third step is planning to achieve that amount of wealth.

What kind of job or activity do you prefer to achieve power?

The fourth step in any successful endeavour involves developing a clear and effective strategy and selecting appropriate methods to achieve the desired goals. This stage is pivotal in guiding the overall direction and execution of the project or plan.

To begin with, crafting a well-thought-out strategy is essential. This entails outlining the overarching approach and vision to accomplish objectives. A comprehensive strategy considers factors such as the organisation's strengths and weaknesses, market dynamics, potential risks, and opportunities. It should align with the overall mission and values of the entity, ensuring that each action taken contributes to the desired outcomes.

Once the strategy is in place, the next critical aspect is selecting the most suitable implementation methods. The chosen methods should align with the strategy, allowing for efficient and effective execution. It is crucial to consider the available resources, time constraints, and the specific context in which the strategy will be carried out.

Moreover, flexibility is key at this stage. As circumstances may change during implementation, the selected methods should be adaptable to accommodate unforeseen challenges or opportunities. This necessitates constant evaluation and monitoring to ensure the chosen methods remain relevant and yield the intended results.

The fifth step is taking action and implementing the chosen method. Now that you have a clear picture of your desired wealth and know how to achieve it, you need to act. Don't be afraid if you have limited resources; start with what you have. As you progress, you will gain more resources and get closer to your goal. However, there may be setbacks and failures along the way. Don't fear failure; it is a part of the journey towards victory.

So, after analysing the word power and finding a correct understanding of it, we should also analyse the word desire. In this section, I didn't analyse wanting; I left it up to you. With only a general explanation, I tried to make it easier for you to redefine the word wanting.

Answer the questions in the table provided to create a suitable roadmap and move towards your goal. Doing so allows you to transform your wishes into specific desires and make them achievable.

1. What is my Financial Goal?	In simple terms, a financial goal is an individual's specific objective regarding money and economic well-being. It could be saving for retirement, buying a house, starting a business, or any other financial aspiration.	
2. How much Wealth do I Need?	Determining the required amount of wealth depends on various factors, such as the chosen	

	financial goal, current lifestyle, and plans. Calculating the necessary funds for achieving the goal is crucial in effective wealth management.	
3. Methods to Achieve the Goal	Multiple approaches or strategies are available to accomplish financial goals. These methods may include saving a portion of income, investing in assets, minimising expenses, and seeking additional sources of income.	
4. Identifying the Best Strategy	The optimal strategy largely depends on individual circumstances, risk tolerance, and time horizon. There is no one-size-fits-all approach, and it is essential to assess different options to	

	find the most suitable one.	
5. Taking the First Step	Initiating the journey towards financial success requires taking the first step. This could involve setting up a budget, starting a savings plan, consulting with a financial advisor, or gaining financial literacy to make informed decisions.	

You must respond to the above questions and analyse them repeatedly to reach the most confident conclusion. Once you have a general plan and outline of your objective, you are ready to proceed with determination. By providing definite answers to the aforementioned questions, you will be like an eagle that spots its prey from high above and swoops down with precision. Undoubtedly, the prey will be in your strong claws.

The lion licks its wounds and continues onward

Controllable and uncontrollable challenges

Some readers may admit that they have identified their goals and tried to achieve them but failed. First, they need to examine their failure in goal-setting and planning. As mentioned above, the goal must be clearly defined with specific details. Secondly, various methods should be carefully examined, and the best ones should be chosen. If someone claims to have followed the above plan and failed, I would advise them to try again. Don't be disheartened; failure is a part of the success process.

Many of us have experienced significant setbacks, and some feel hopeless, believing that gaining financial or any other form of power is impossible. Our wounds have become more important than ourselves, and we are sorrowful. However, one must know that hopelessness is the greatest wound of all. It consumes us before we die. We must be like lions. Lions get wounded many times throughout their lives. Severe wounds that would quickly kill a hopeless lion, but lions never lose hope. They lick their wounds and continue on their way. Instead of focusing on their wounds, they concentrate on their goals. When we focus on our goals, we even forget the pain of our wounds. Celebrating the most minor successes teaches us to be joyful instead of complaining, gradually changing our way of life and bringing us closer to a source of strength. A person who is tired and defeated will only become more exhausted even by reading this book unless they decide right now to leave their complaints behind. I love the philosophy of the **Stoics**. They believed we could have two approaches to events: either we can control them or not. So, if the event is controllable, there is no need to complain; we should take control of it. And if it is uncontrollable, complaining won't change anything because it won't affect the outcome. **Seneca** was one of the Stoic philosophers. The Roman Emperor **Nero** ordered his execution, and Seneca accepted it without sorrow. He knew there was no possibility of escaping Nero's order, and complaining wouldn't affect Nero's executioners, who were sent to kill him, so he accepted the decision without any grief. Nero ordered him to commit suicide, and he tried various methods to end his life. He even drank poison like **Socrates**, but he didn't die. Yet, he didn't give up and managed to end his life eventually. He couldn't control Nero's executioners to spare his life, so complaining and crying wouldn't change his fate. Therefore, he accepted the outcome, but he never accepted defeat. Trump might have appeared frail at 77, but he continued his struggle. Even though he might have never heard the term "Stoicism," his actions were precisely that. He did what **Albert Ellis** and **Carl Rogers**, psychologists, recommended to their clients.

Our failures don't have to be as significant as Trump's defeat in the 2020 presidential election. The magnitude of any failure is proportionate to an individual's possessions. If someone loses a significant portion of their possessions, they might be defeated. These possessions could be their credibility, job, spouse, or home. For example, if an employee loses their job for some reason and can't repay the bank loan they took to buy a house, the bank will seize their home. We can frame their failure as follows: 1- Losing the job 2- Losing the home 3- Causing family conflicts 4- Divorce and potentially losing their children. These wounds are powerful enough to knock a lion off its feet, but Stoics resist all of them. The question is, what should they do? Stoics say: Sit down and think. Yes, think! The most important thing one should do in this stage is to seek refuge within oneself to find a way out of the impasse. Thinking can save us. At this point, one should not act because problems are like quicksand; the more we struggle, the deeper we sink. So, first, we need to maintain our calmness and think. Positive thinking is the only way to salvation.

You can say I have lost everything, but I still have other things I can find hope in. I may have lost my possessions, but my essence continues. I am still present, and this existence has the potential to rebuild everything anew. I haven't lost my inherent abilities; I can still speak, read, write, move, breathe, and connect with others. I am still a father or mother to my children, and they are waiting for the wounded lion to rise again on its feet. In this situation, there are no more options: I either succumb to the intensity of my wounds, or I endure the pain and stand up again. The choice is mine.

As the philosophers used to say, "If you can control, do so; if you cannot, accept it." I must assess what aspects are within my control in this situation where I've lost most of my life's facilities. It's natural to feel sorrow, anger, and helplessness; weaker individuals may let these emotions consume them to alleviate their pain. They either succumb to their suffering or find ways to overcome it and rise again. They reflect upon themselves, identifying their weaknesses in their previous jobs. If their weaknesses were within their control, they would reconsider their behaviour. If their weaknesses depend on others, they forget them, as others become victims of their beliefs.

Now, they ponder over their abilities. If they were employees, which specific skills were most in demand in their previous role? Whether in a company, administration, or factory, they list these skills on paper. For instance, suppose they were an executive manager. This job requires strong public relations, effective social connections, management skills, fostering communication between different departments, and effective time management. This person undoubtedly possessed numerous capabilities, which made the company employ them. Now, they have a more precise understanding of their abilities.

Next, they identify companies and factories that need these skills. Many companies and organisations require solid executive managers. They prepare an outstanding resume and send it to dozens of companies. Then, like a lion waiting for its prey, they patiently await the right opportunity. Eventually, one of the companies responds and expresses their readiness to hire them. The first step towards reclaiming their lost job has succeeded. Now, they have a job and can repay their bank loan. What's the next step? Yes, I am negotiating with the bank.

In your mind, envision this story. If you encounter any obstacles, write them down and find solutions. Overcoming difficulties is as simple as writing them down here. However, weak individuals tend to magnify the obstacles and inadvertently declare their definitive failure before participating in the competition.

The philosophers, known as Stoicism, had three fundamental beliefs. They said to control external events, you must control your thoughts. (Human-oriented psychologists like **Carl Rogers** and **Albert Ellis** have registered the idea of Stoicism under their names!)

The first principle is that some things are within our control while others are not. Most of our unhappiness arises from mistakenly believing we have control over things we don't. So, if you have previously failed in achieving your goal, examine the reasons and write them down in the table below to organise your thoughts and find a solution.

Failures	Controllable Reasons	Uncontrollable Reasons	Post-Failure Actions	Controlling Controllable Reasons	**Achieving Success**
Failures can occur for various reasons, including controllable and uncontrollable factors. Identifying these reasons and taking appro	Controllable reasons are those factors that are within our control, and their management can significantly impact the outcome. These reasons can	After experiencing a failure, it is crucial to take corrective actions to learn from the experience and improve future endeavours. Conducting a thorough post-mortem analysi	By effectively controlling the controllable reasons, individuals or organizations can enhance their chances of success. This	By addressing failures appropriately and taking measures to control controllable reasons, individuals and organizations pave the way for	

priate post-failure actions are essential to achieving success.	include inadequate planning, lack of resources, or insufficient skills.	s, seeking feedback, and making necessary adjustments are some of the actions that can help in this process.	entails careful planning, efficient resource allocation, skill development, and proactive risk management.	achieving success in their endeavours. Success can be defined by reaching desired goals, attaining objectives, and accomplishing missions with positive outcomes.	

Before reading this book, you might have pondered the reasons for failure, but you haven't distinguished between controllable and uncontrollable reasons. Therefore, if you wish to complete the above table, you can only fill in the first four columns. However, after reading this book, you can fill in the last two columns: "Controlling Controllable Reasons" and "Achieving Success." Once you have control over manageable reasons, you will undoubtedly achieve success. I hope that soon, using the approach I have presented, you can fill in the last column, the success column.

The limitations of human control

The concept of control, as discussed by the philosopher **Epicurus**, revolves around the idea that we possess limited influence over various aspects of our lives. Events that unfold around us, the actions and words of others, and even the vulnerabilities of our own bodies lie beyond our direct control. The true sphere of control, according to Epicurus, resides in our thoughts and judgments concerning the world, including our perceptions of people, objects, and the environment as a whole. However, I present an alternative perspective: the potential for complete control over everything, attainable through mastery of our minds. By cultivating control over our thoughts, we can influence our entire experience. Consider the example of a merchant who loses all possessions due to war. Initially, amidst the chaos of war, the merchant has little control over external events. Yet, by harnessing control over the mind, different outcomes emerge.

One scenario involves the mind succumbing to despair and hopelessness, viewing the loss as insurmountable. Such a belief may lead to depression, isolation, or worse, self-destructive tendencies. In contrast, another outlook emerges, perceiving wealth as non-defining and seeking resilience. In this case, the individual heals emotional wounds and moves forward, displaying strength and adaptability. While the best-case scenario may not result in the complete recovery of lost wealth, a sense of fulfilment and determination to thrive characterise this mindset. Thus, while some philosophical perspectives may emphasise limited control, mastering one's mind as the gateway to overall control holds significant value. By mastery over our thoughts and beliefs, we attain influence over various facets of existence. Such an argument stands as an exceptional and empowering stance.

Let's reconsider the central theme once again, emphasising the principle of accepting that we cannot control everything. As we delve into this concept, take a moment to reflect on its implications and how it may impact your perspective while reading this book. Consider whether accepting this principle brings comfort and helps you come to terms with failures beyond your control. Now, let's explore your past setbacks and failures, those moments that seemed to immobilise you and strip away your sense of control. Ask yourself if you could have prevented these failures. If the answer is negative, accepting them and acknowledging that they were beyond your control becomes easier. However, if your response is affirmative, acknowledging that you could have prevented the failure due to accurate calculation, it marks a positive step forward.

The next question is crucial: Can you now control the mistakes you've made to minimise further damage? In Iran, there's a saying: "Preventing harm wherever possible is beneficial!" This proverb emphasises the importance of recognising and correcting mistakes when they are within our control. For example, if you lost your spouse due to excessive pessimism and demanding behaviour, acknowledging this as a controllable failure is essential. Now, the focus should be on controlling your behaviour and emotions after the separation. To achieve this, consider seeking help from a psychologist and investing in self-improvement. By taking these steps, you regain a sense of control over your actions and emotions. You may even choose to reach out to your former spouse, apologise, and explain the role your paranoia played in the relationship's demise. This step signifies growth and reclaiming control over your life.

However, it's crucial to recognise that there are aspects beyond your control, such as your spouse moving on and entering another relationship. Despite your efforts to change and correct mistakes, the outcomes of others' decisions remain outside your sphere of influence. Having read this book and delving into Stoic strategies, you will accept that some relationships have ended, and you must embrace the idea of a fresh start. The significant difference now is that you have transformed. You know what you can control and what lies beyond your influence. You haven't ignored your mistakes; rather, you have acknowledged controllable events and made progress in correcting them. With this newfound understanding, if you decide to embark on a new relationship or remarry, you can do so with the wisdom you gained from your experiences. Armed with this knowledge of what you can control, you can avoid falling into the same mistakes and approach your future with a sense of empowerment and resilience. Remember, we cannot control everything, but we can control our responses and actions, making a profound difference in navigating life's challenges.

This topic delves into the profound teachings of Epictetus, highlighting the second fundamental principle of his philosophy. According to Epictetus, our unhappiness is not caused by external circumstances or the actions of others but rather by the way we think about these events. When events occur, we tend to pass judgment on them, shaping our emotional responses. For instance, we may experience unhappiness, sadness, or anger if we perceive something as genuinely wrong. On the other hand, if we anticipate adverse outcomes, we may feel fear. These emotions are not inherent in the events themselves; rather, they arise from our judgments about the events. It is essential to recognise that events are morally neutral. What may be distressing to one person might be inconsequential or even welcome to another. The value we assign to these events through our judgments gives rise to our emotional reactions. This understanding underscores the significance of our thought processes in shaping our emotional well-being. The concept of the link between thoughts and emotions is also emphasised in Rational Emotive Behaviour Therapy (REBT). This therapeutic approach emphasises that our beliefs greatly influence our emotions. Hence, embracing the idea that emotions are not external but intimately connected to our beliefs is crucial. When we hold beliefs that foster feelings of helplessness, emotions like fear, shame, and inadequacy can take hold of us. Conversely, positive emotions are more likely to prevail when we perceive ourselves as capable individuals. Believing in our own powerlessness can trigger the second emotion - sadness or depression. To illustrate the thought process, we can understand that our emotions are deeply intertwined with our beliefs about ourselves, others, and the world around us. Recognising this connection empowers us to evaluate and challenge our beliefs, fostering a healthier and more positive emotional state.

In essence, Epictetus's teachings and the principles of REBT remind us of our power over our emotional responses. We can cultivate a more resilient and contented outlook on life by critically examining and reshaping our thought patterns and beliefs. The journey toward emotional well-being lies in understanding the role of our judgments and beliefs and consciously choosing to cultivate a positive and empowering mindset.

Many psychologists often fail to discern between events within our control and those beyond our control in the cycle of events. This oversight can lead many clients to blame themselves or others unjustly during multiple counselling sessions. However, if individuals comprehend the concept of control and uncontrollability concerning an event, they would refrain from self-blame or blaming others. Some psychologists, particularly counsellors, focus on an individual's core beliefs and behaviours before addressing their actions. While this approach may have some merits, it also burdens the individual heavily. Therefore, when someone seeks assistance due to a specific event, it is essential first to examine the events and ascertain their role. Finding a solution becomes more manageable if they have no involvement in the event. For example, suppose someone blames themselves for their spouse's accident. In that case, it is crucial to identify their actual role in the accident carefully. By objectively presenting the facts and relevant factors, the person can realise that they either had no role in the accident or their involvement was minimal. Adopting this method allows us to focus on success and move forward constructively.

In analysing the life of Donald Trump, we find an individual who seemingly grasps this concept of controllable and uncontrollable events intuitively without having studied various psychology books. Looking at Trump's political life, he had no political or military experience in his resume. However, he confidently pursued high-risk projects and various business ventures, demonstrating his self-belief and confidence in his abilities. Trump's life also illustrates that he has faced failures in some of his projects. For instance, "Trump Airlines," a venture he acquired in 1988 with a $245 million loan, failed after two years, leading him to relinquish ownership to his creditors. Despite the setback, Trump quickly recognised that he had no control over external factors that dictated the project's fate. By gracefully surrendering, he could redirect his focus to other endeavours and achieve success in different areas. This ability to surrender gracefully was, in fact, a significant triumph, as it prevented him from enduring even greater losses. Trump's success as a businessman lies in his understanding of uncontrollable events and knowing when to let go and turn a situation into a victory rather than a defeat.

Based on this principle, it becomes crucial to identify controllable events in our own lives. Recognising what is within our control is vital for personal growth and success. Many people spend their lives lamenting over things they have lost control over when, instead, an intelligent approach would be to acknowledge their limitations and work within those boundaries. Emphasising our strengths and abilities enables us to move forward, even in the face of failure, without ending in endless grief. Therefore, there is a need to correct the cycle described earlier, which does not differentiate between controllable and uncontrollable events. By making this small but significant adjustment, we can take another step closer to achieving success in our endeavours. Recognising the boundaries of our control allows us to navigate life with greater wisdom and resilience, ultimately leading us towards a path of personal growth and achievement.

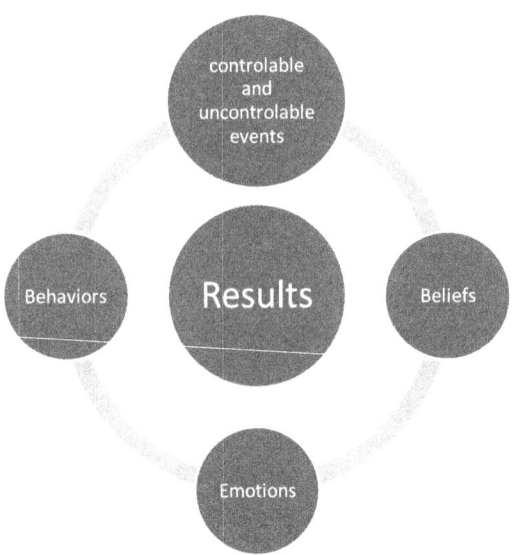

Events are not the only things that are sometimes beyond our control. Often, people's reactions, behaviours, and words prove to be uncontrollable. This principle holds great significance and is repeatedly evident in Trump's life - the impact of people's words. A successful individual may have numerous opponents, but those who adopt a Stoic mindset, believing that external circumstances and others' actions cannot disturb them, remain unaffected by people's words. This brings us to the second crucial principle: it is our own thoughts that lead to our distress, not the behaviours of others. Control, or rather the lack thereof, becomes a central theme. We cannot control every individual we encounter. Even the most accomplished individuals will inevitably face opposition and discontent. To progress towards gaining power, we must recognise the limits of our influence and identify the uncontrollable factors that hinder our path to empowerment. Understanding what is within our control and beyond allows us to navigate the path more accurately. Without such comprehension, we risk repeatedly striving for power only to encounter defeat.

Lions do not become cats by mocking

Marcus Aurelius had a unique strategy to approach each day. He would remind himself in the morning that he might encounter people who were under immense stress, angry, impatient, or ungrateful. He hoped to respond differently than those around him by mentally preparing for such situations beforehand. However, Marcus Aurelius also recognised that these individuals were not intentionally behaving this way; they were influenced by their own misguided judgments. Earlier, we discussed controlling certain events while accepting others as beyond our control. Now, let's focus on individual behaviour. Just as external events can affect our mental well-being, the actions of people we know or strangers can also influence our lives. To achieve success, it is crucial to understand human behaviour and interactions. Marcus Aurelius's strategy is essential in this regard. He demonstrated the importance of adapting our responses when faced with purposeful, angry, or rude individuals, enabling us to navigate such situations successfully.

Two principles come into play here. The first involves taking control of our own minds and behaviour. The second principle entails viewing those exhibiting negative behaviour as victims of their own false beliefs and judgments rather than simply wrongdoers. By adopting this mindset, we free ourselves from reacting in the same negative manner.

This approach opens the path to success, preventing others from trapping us in negative emotions and hindering our potential achievements. Changing our core beliefs boosts our self-worth and empowers us to acquire valuable skills and abilities. As I mentioned earlier, the power of our existence lies within our control, even for those facing disabilities. Our minds are shaped by beliefs, and the stronger and more rational these beliefs become, the more powerful our sense of self will be. True strength, as demonstrated by individuals like Marcus Aurelius, does not solely come from wealth or political and financial power. It emanates from having resilient and unwavering beliefs compared to others. To succeed, we must strengthen our self-existence and nurture a positive and empowering mindset.

Donald Trump has faced consistent criticism and mockery from comedians, targeting aspects of his speech, appearance, and hairstyle. Reputable American newspapers have also questioned his worldview on numerous occasions. Additionally, his behaviour towards his family has been under scrutiny, with some making claims about his relationship with his daughter. Despite these remarks, Trump remained steadfast and unaffected, understanding that his own mindset determined whether he would be upset or not. He recognised that people would always gossip and accuse, but he chose not to invest his time and energy in such negativity. Trump's ability to maintain composure amidst criticism exemplifies the profound impact of our thoughts on our emotions. By cultivating positive thinking, we can foster positive emotions, freeing ourselves from anger, hatred, and sorrow. Changing one's behaviour is no simple task, as family and societal influences shape it. Negative emotions can be acquired from our immediate environment. For example, if a person's father responded to situations with anger and shouting due to addiction, the individual might learn to react with anger even to minor incidents or objections. To achieve success in life, it is essential to identify the influences that have shaped our beliefs and develop emotional literacy to manage our emotions effectively in various situations. Failure to navigate this process can lead to numerous challenges and eventual failure. While some individuals with high levels of negative emotions may seem successful on the surface, closer examination often reveals otherwise. A boss who exhibits nervousness and aggression but owns multiple large companies may be wealthy but not truly successful. They may experience broken family relationships, troubled interpersonal connections, and a yearning for genuine human connection. Even in the workplace, such individuals may act as dictators, commanding their employees but failing to earn genuine respect. Subordinates might contemplate leaving if they had the same benefits offered elsewhere, illustrating that power and wealth cannot secure loyalty when it is accompanied by hostility. These individuals may hold double standards, showing anger towards those weaker than them but acting submissive in the presence of more powerful individuals, fearing the loss of resources and privileges. These beliefs and false assumptions fuel their negative emotions. Dictators, in essence, feel threatened and exert control over weaker individuals while attempting to placate those with greater power. This dual standard hamper their success and happiness.

To counteract these negative behaviours, individuals must better understand mutual behaviour. Treating people respectfully is important, but they should not allow others to manipulate their emotions. Maintaining inner calm and focusing on personal growth and success is crucial, rather than getting upset over someone else's inappropriate actions. If needed, efforts to change their behaviour can be made, but if they prove unchangeable and harmful, it is better to leave such environments with positive emotions intact. Ultimately, maintaining emotional composure empowers individuals to be their own boss and not be swayed by external influences. Like a lion, one must remain steadfast and true to themselves, not allowing ridicule to alter their essence.

The Angry Lion Only Hurts

Once we acknowledge our inherent power, view failures as stepping stones to success, and gain a clear understanding of what we can control and what we cannot, our emotions find balance. Before grasping these insights, we often find ourselves trapped in feelings of depression, anger, or hopelessness. However, armed with this newfound comprehension, our emotions become better aligned with our true selves and the world around us. Regulating our emotions and replacing negative feelings with positive ones open the path to progress and growth.

As mentioned earlier, emotional awareness precedes the cognitive aspect, which is equally vital. Without cognitive understanding, the other dimensions hold little meaning. In the cognitive dimension, we come to realise that not everything is within our control, but our minds are malleable. Hence, we can learn to accept even life's most profound tragedies by controlling our thoughts and transcending the shape of catastrophe. This cognitive dimension paves the way for positive emotions to take root in our minds. The transformation in the cognitive dimension also triggers changes in the physiological dimension, making us feel physically capable. While negative emotions like fear, anger, or helplessness might lead to physical symptoms such as heart palpitations, anxiety, or paralysis, positive emotions empower us physically. Those who have altered their cognitive beliefs, gained control over their thoughts, nurtured positive convictions, and experienced improved physiological responses will also exhibit more constructive behaviour. In essence, the third dimension is the behavioural dimension. Each emotion sets off a pattern of behaviours within us. When we feel angry, we may react by yelling, arguing, or engaging in nervous habits. However, such ineffective behaviours do not lead us to success. On the other hand, positive emotions inspire us to behave in a more composed, respectful, and goal-oriented manner.

Our judgments in mutual behaviour are founded on our beliefs. When we hold human dignity in high regard and recognise the fallibility of others, we become less prone to getting upset or negatively judging mistakes. In such instances, positive emotions are experienced, and our behaviour is designed accordingly. The good news is that we have complete control over our value judgments. Events occur, and inherently, they are neither good nor bad. It lies within our power to decide how we perceive and value them.

The Stoics' paradox, beautifully formulated by Epictetus, reminds us that while we might hardly control external circumstances, we do possess the power to govern our own happiness. The Stoics developed a comprehensive set of practical exercises to apply these Stoic principles in everyday life and cultivate them further. Seneca recommended evaluating, recording, and reflecting on daily actions at the end of each day. By doing so, we become aware of the trivial things that caused us distress during the day or how our angry behaviour in response to someone else's actions, which did not warrant such a reaction, negatively impacted us. Through daily evaluation and recording, Seneca hoped we would act better the next day, learning and growing from each experience. Epictetus wisely advises that we will be disappointed if we expect the world to conform to our desires. However, if we learn to accept whatever the world offers, we can lead a smoother and happier life.

In this section, we come across a paradox: while no one actively chooses to experience emotions like sadness, stress, anger, or resentment, these states are actually shaped by our judgments. The only aspect we have control over is our judgments. If we believe that things should always go our way and that any deviation from our desires is unacceptable, we end up feeling disturbed. Similarly, if we believe that we are highly valuable and should not be insulted by others, we will become angry when faced with criticism. It becomes evident that our beliefs significantly influence our emotions, which in turn affect our behaviour. Thus, it can be said that we are essentially defined by our beliefs. As discussed earlier, self-absorbed individuals tend to view the world as revolving around them, leading them to take themselves too seriously and, consequently, experience depression. However, intelligent individuals understand that nothing in the world is so inherently valuable that it warrants biased attachment, not even themselves. When faced with insults or humiliation, they do not immediately react with anger because they do not attribute excessive importance to their own image. They do not allow anyone to criticise or insult them overly. This highlights the third Stoic strategy: not taking oneself too seriously!

Now, let's take a moment to reflect on the changes within us since we began reading this book. To help us grasp this, let's review the two tables below.

Before reading the book			
An adverse incident leads to failure.	A central belief related to failure	Emotions associated with the central belief	The consequences of negative emotions
dismissal from work	1- I am disabled 2- I have no supply	sorrow depression anger hate	Continuation of failure and its distribution in other parts of life and becoming a

	3- I am unlucky	Isolation	person who always loses
	4- The employer is unfair		
	5- The employer is ungrateful		

After reading the book				
An adverse incident leads to failure.	A central belief related to failure	Analysis of central beliefs	Emotions related to analysis	Consequences of positive emotions
dismissal from work	1- Accepting indivi	My individual mistakes	happiness	Find a new job avoid past mistakes,

114

	dual mistakes	are controllable	Hope The will to correct	and become a winner
	2 - Accepting the biased behaviour of the employer	The employer's biased behaviour is uncontrollable		

It is that straightforward. When we acknowledge our inherent abilities and perceive our mistakes as opportunities for growth while identifying controllable factors, we naturally adopt a more positive outlook, leading to changes in our behaviour. With a newfound sense of hope, we approach problem-solving with determination instead of giving up. So, if you've encountered failure multiple times, it simply means you haven't followed the process effectively. Review everything again, pinpoint the issues, and make the necessary adjustments to steer your life towards a better path. Grab a piece of paper, create two tables similar to the ones mentioned earlier, jot down your past failures, and analyse your problem-solving approach using the provided example.

The lion also dies

Everything is mortal

Nothing in the world possesses permanent validity. All worldly credibility is finite. In the best-case scenario, an individual can live for a hundred years, after which significant ambiguity will ensue. This reality may instil humility in us. A person aware of their limited existence, unable to hinder the ageing process, shall not harbour prejudices towards anything in the universe. They will recognise that everything shall perish within a short period. No power endures eternally. All things are destined for decay; sooner or later, they cease to exist. This applies to the entirety of planet Earth as well. Thus, while striving for power, we must also have faith in its impermanence, which enables spiritual growth and enhances our acquisitive abilities.

The third strategy of Stoics advises us to remember our relative insignificance. The world does not revolve around us. Emperor Marcus Aurelius, seeking to place his short life in a broader context, contemplated incessantly upon the greatness and vastness of the universe, extending from the past to the future. When our lives are viewed from a cosmic perspective, they are mere fleeting moments. In light of this, why should we expect the cosmos to grant us our desires? The expectation that the world should align with our wishes is foolish. Epictetus asserts that we will be disappointed if we expect the world to give us what we want. However, accepting whatever the world provides will lead to a smoother and more contented life. Uttering these words is more manageable than embodying them in practice, yet more and more individuals embrace Stoic principles and strive to implement them in their everyday lives. Some individuals misinterpret a particular approach to the material world in certain religious and mystical beliefs. They draw from Stoic arguments and divine scriptures to argue that humans should refrain from accumulating worldly possessions as insignificant beings. However, their interpretation of this strategy is flawed. Being insignificant does not mean we should not strive to build meaningful lives. As I mentioned earlier, according to Maslow's hierarchy of needs, humans must pursue a fulfilling life in their specific era, embracing the beauty and best aspects it offers, while remaining resilient if they lose or fail to attain certain things. Material possessions do not define our worth, so their loss should not bring sorrow. This perspective enriches our spiritual understanding, preventing us from becoming slaves to materialism, even if we achieve wealth. If we possess the power to control physical or mental challenges, we should do so without hesitation. But when we lack that control, we must face these difficulties with resilience and perseverance on our chosen path. Let's be honest: if we choose to wallow in self-pity, we only weaken ourselves and lose touch with our inner strength. On the other hand, embracing strength empowers us to continue our journey with determination.

By thoroughly reviewing the contents of this chapter, we shed light on the path ahead. Armed with enlightened knowledge, we confidently step forward on our journey through life.

Chapter Summary

In this chapter, we explored the concept of inherent power within every individual. By recognising and respecting this inherent power, we can harness it to develop additional strengths and achieve success. Determination is a vital factor in pursuing success, allowing us to overcome failures and setbacks.

Security and tranquillity are universal desires, and perseverance makes them attainable for all. Embracing failure as an inevitable part of the journey, successful individuals focus on controlling what they can and accepting what is beyond their control. Understanding the impact of beliefs on emotions and behaviour, they modify distorted or negative beliefs to align their actions with their aspirations.

The significance of healthy beliefs as the primary power cannot be overstated. Relying on this inherent power is key to acquiring additional strengths. Mistaken beliefs can lead to negative emotions and irrational behaviours, hindering progress. To maintain perspective, we should remember that life holds more value than material possessions. By strengthening our spiritual beliefs and letting go of material attachments, we can govern objects and possessions instead of being governed by them. We must translate theoretical knowledge into practical behaviours to derive value from this chapter. After repeatedly reading and internalising the content, we should identify and correct deficiencies in our cognition, emotions, or beliefs to achieve the desired outcomes.

Now, let's reflect on the following questions:

1. Are you aware of your inherent powers? If so, please name them.

2. Do you utilise your inherent powers to acquire additional strengths? If yes, explain how.

3. Have you discovered creative methods, relying on your inherent powers, to reach acquired strengths? If not, when do you intend to find them?

4. Do you surrender when facing failure or start anew? What are the reasons if you surrender, and how can you overcome them?

5. Do you differentiate between controllable and uncontrollable reasons for your failures?

6. Do you understand that failure is a natural process of every success?

7. Do you possess the ability to identify false beliefs and correct them?

Now that you have answered the above questions let's move forward:

A: What goals have you set for your future?

B: Which inherent power will accompany you in achieving your objectives?

C: How will you benefit from your powers in reaching your goals?

Congratulations on taking these steps towards success and navigating the path with wisdom. With determination and understanding of your inherent power, you are well on your way to achieving your objectives. Stay committed, and success will be within your rea

Chapter 2
Wanting

Power concedes nothing without a demand. It never did, and it never will

Frederick Douglass

Reboot your brain

When you discover your mission, you will feel its demand. It will fill you with enthusiasm and a burning desire to get to work on it.

W. Clement Stone

When the mind has encountered failure repeatedly, the path to success can feel elusive and unattainable. In such instances, a crucial step is to reset one's approach to achieve the desired outcome. A brain that has grown accustomed to failure struggles to comprehend the idea of victory. Therefore, if you genuinely intend to reach your goal this time, you must first rewire your own brain. While it would be convenient to purchase a new brain from the market, such an option is not feasible, leaving us with the task of reloading our existing brain to serve our ambitions. To support this argument, I turn to a significant psychological experiment by **Martin Seligman**, which aimed to demonstrate that the human brain can become conditioned even to helplessness and habitual failure. This ground-breaking study earned Seligman the prestigious Nobel Prize.

Seligman's experiment involved training 20 Shih Tzu dogs from infancy in a cage with a pedal that allowed them to exit and return after relieving themselves. The dogs were then divided into two groups, each consisting of 10. In the experiment (Cage B), Seligman electrified the floor and subjected the dogs to electric shocks three times a day for 30 days. Initially, the dogs reacted to the shocks by attempting to escape, resulting in injuries as they hit the door. However, after several days of repeated shocks and unsuccessful escape attempts, they reached a point of **learned helplessness**, where they came to believe that their efforts were futile, leading them to give up trying. Even when Seligman later opened the door of Cage B and allowed them to go to the control group cage (Cage A) with a door that could be opened by pushing a lever, the dogs showed no interest in leaving. They had become conditioned to their sense of helplessness. The only learning the dogs acquired was to stand still and avoid hitting the poles during the shocks to minimise injury. Their brains had convinced them that escape from the cage was impossible. They lost the inclination for "seeking" and instead focused on staying still to avoid harm, leading them into a state of misery.

As we have already explored in the previous section, recognising the powers within us is the first step toward achieving our goals. However, it is essential to understand that merely possessing sufficient power is not enough; we must also know what we truly want. For instance, someone might possess tremendous physical strength, but their power goes to waste without understanding their desires. I have encountered many individuals with impressive physical prowess yet lacking a clear sense of direction; they use their strength for manual labour. Influenced by societal expectations, family pressures, and cultural norms, they believe their strength is valuable only for such tasks, and they resign themselves to this notion. While they may have discovered their physical strength, they have not grasped the stage of "wanting" or aspiring to higher pursuits. Becoming a renowned shipbuilder or weightlifter never crosses their minds, and any such ambitions are ridiculed and disapproved. The central philosophy of this book is redefining words. As you can see, people who fail continuously have a negative definition of success. They do not see themselves as worthy of success or blame external factors for their failure. Therefore, redefining the word "success" is very important. With the techniques mentioned in the first chapter, you should redefine the word success. Understand the role of external factors. Identify how to overcome external factors and have a correct definition of success. To redefine it, you need to identify your most minor achievements to realise that you have achieved many achievements and can continue to achieve more. Gradually, these individuals lose hope for greater achievements, and their demand for more attainable powers diminishes as they settle for mundane work.

In essence, the emotions and feelings of someone who has fallen into hopelessness are akin to those observed in the dogs from Seligman's experiment. Similarly, the sentiments of someone who remains uncertain about their life's desires also share parallels with those of these dogs. To break free from this flawed cycle, we must embark on the journey of identifying what we truly seek. If your brain persistently instils the belief that success is unattainable, it deceives you, altering the very locus of your ambitions and redirecting you from striving for success toward accepting failure. To liberate yourself from this mental entrapment, you must undertake the task of reconfiguring your brain anew. In this chapter, you will confront your own mind, preparing yourself for the most challenging battle that lies ahead. The transformation that awaits you is essential to reclaiming control of your thoughts and setting yourself to achieve your goals and dreams.

Are you a lion or a fox? Make a decision!

Not everyone aspires to be wealthy, knowledgeable, famous, or powerful. Some individuals find contentment in leading a simple life driven by their personal beliefs. **Alfred Adler**, a prominent psychologist, emphasised that individual lifestyles are shaped by the cultural influences in which people are raised. As a result, various lifestyles, such as the Western, single, and religious lifestyles, emerge as people choose based on their beliefs and circumstances. The pursuit of power, whether material, spiritual, social, or political, depends on an individual's values and convictions. Those who lean towards a minimalist and ascetic life are not enticed by the allure of worldly powers. For instance, Buddhists prioritise elevating their spiritual power rather than accumulating financial wealth.

To illustrate the impact of personal beliefs on one's life, let's delve into the intriguing story of **Bodhidharma**, the Buddhist monk credited with bringing Zen Buddhism to China. Bodhidharma's unique approach to teaching was characterised by prolonged meditation, leaving a lasting impression on those around him. His spiritual journey led him to the Shaolin Monastery, where he introduced martial arts to the monks after witnessing their physical weaknesses. Similarly, **Diogenes**, a renowned cynic philosopher, adopted a lifestyle of extreme simplicity and sought to challenge societal norms through his unconventional behaviour. He lived in a clay barrel, possessed only a cloak and staff, and practised begging from statues to overcome the fear of rejection. He aimed to open people's eyes to the cultural norms that dictated their lives. While these examples prompt reflection, it's essential to recognise that living simply does not equate to living in poverty. One can lead a minimalist lifestyle while possessing significant wealth, utilising it for charitable purposes or promoting knowledge and education. This chapter focuses on individuals who have chosen contentment with minimal wealth and lack a desire for further accumulation of power. Understanding one's desires and lifestyle is influenced by the society and family they were raised in, along with their core beliefs. Different religions and cultural backgrounds also shape individual aspirations. In capitalist societies, the pursuit of material wealth is often emphasised, leading to a common desire for financial acquisition. It becomes crucial to identify personal values, analyse beliefs, and act accordingly to align one's actions with one's intellectual background. Furthermore, recognising one's personality type plays a significant role in understanding desires and aspirations. Introverted individuals may have distinct desires compared to extroverted personalities.

Self-awareness is critical to comprehending one's preferences; various online personality tests can aid in this process. This book addresses general questions with the assumption that all human beings share commonalities. Individuals can better understand themselves by answering these general questions and delving into specific coordinates. In the first step towards self-discovery, it is vital to determine whether one gravitates towards a life akin to that of a wealthy person or that of a person with modest means. Knowing oneself on this fundamental level will guide individuals to fulfilment and contentment.

Do you prefer poverty or wealth?

Whether one prefers poverty or wealth can be intricate, often reflecting a conflict within oneself. Many people have noticed that two distinct personas seem to coexist within them—one with a fervent desire for wealth and success and the other content with simplicity and minimal possessions. This duality resonates with me; I believe it is an essential aspect of our inner psyche. **Eric Berne's** theory of three faces and identities—Child, Adult, and Parent—further emphasises the complexity of our existence. Although I won't delve deep into Berne's theory, I aim to prompt you to confront your true self. Our upbringing plays a vital role in shaping our inclinations and core values. Whether we grew up in a family or under the care of someone else, their way of life and beliefs have significantly influenced us, often at a subconscious level. For instance, my father led a simple life and displayed little interest in wealth. His contentment with the bare minimum left a profound impression on me during my formative years. Consequently, an internal conflict emerged within me. On the one hand, I yearned for financial success, while on the other, my subconscious echoed my father's voice, advocating contentment with less. This psychological phenomenon is called Approach-Approach Conflict, where one feels pulled in opposing directions. For me, the pull towards simplicity and contentment overshadowed the desire for wealth for a long time, and I took no action to achieve prosperity.

It was only after becoming a psychologist and delving into my own life that I recognised the influence of my father's voice in my subconscious, repeatedly advising, "Be content with the minimum." This revelation allowed me to understand the source of my internal conflict and why I had previously resisted wealth-building opportunities. For you, too, it is crucial to introspect and identify the voices within yourself that may be holding you back from embracing prosperity. These voices could stem from religious or philosophical beliefs. The key lies in recognising and differentiating between conflicting inclinations. On the other hand, if someone genuinely lacks the desire to become wealthy, they should not feel pressured by societal expectations to pursue material riches. Some individuals find self-sufficiency and contentment in modest circumstances and are free from dependence on material possessions. This quality of self-sufficiency enhances their identity, and they are not driven by the pursuit of wealth. In contrast, some billionaires become so attached to their wealth that they feel uneasy about parting with even a small amount. These individuals are not truly wealthy;

they are held captive by their need for material possessions.

Hence, the first step in this journey is self-discovery. Understand who you are and whether you genuinely desire wealth or not. If your answer leans towards contentment with less, there is no need to reproach yourself or feel pressured to pursue material success. Embrace the quality of self-sufficiency and enjoy the beauty of life in its simplicity. However, if the desire for wealth resides within you, this exploration has only just begun. It is essential to understand and confront the conflicting voices within yourself and pave the way towards achieving your aspirations.

Understanding Our Desires: Exploring the Path to Prosperity

Understanding our deepest inclinations and discovering genuine happiness and contentment are profound and essential quests. While these questions may initially seem daunting, it is crucial to confront them honestly and fearlessly. Take a moment to reflect: Have you ever felt disheartened and melancholic, dwelling on perceived shortcomings in your daily life or over an extended period? Do you occasionally feel inadequate, comparing yourself to those with greater power and wealth, leading to feelings of insufficiency? Or perhaps you have justified remaining in a state of financial scarcity, unable to break free from its grip?

If any of these scenarios resonate with you, you may grapple with an internal double standard demanding recognition. To progress and find true fulfilment, it is vital to identify your genuine needs and desires. As you embark on this journey, allow yourself the space and time to discern the various inner voices that inhabit your mind. Distinguish between your authentic voice, the one that speaks from your heart and reflects your true essence, and the voices of external influences, such as those of your parents, guardians, or religious leaders. By recognising these distinct voices, you can begin to assign significance to your own convictions while gradually silencing the external ones.

As you explore further, it is essential to gain awareness of the external factors that have influenced these voices, shaping your beliefs and perspectives. Identify the societal norms, cultural pressures, and conditioning that may have shaped your thought patterns over time. By acknowledging these influences, you can then start the process of gradually disentangling yourself from their hold, allowing your authentic self to emerge. Embrace this process with patience and self-compassion, for it is not an overnight transformation. Embracing your true self and detaching from external expectations requires courage and resilience. However, as you make progress, you will embark on a path towards personal growth, self-discovery, and prosperity in all its forms.

Remember, this is a journey unique to you, and the destination is not a final endpoint but an ongoing process of evolution and self-awareness. Allow yourself the freedom to explore, question, and learn along the way. Trust that you will uncover the keys to your own prosperity and profound contentment by uncovering your genuine needs and desires. May this voyage of self-discovery lead you to a life of authenticity, purpose, and fulfilment.

Double standards are the enemy of successful

In pursuing wealth, it is essential to recognise and address the psychological aspects that may hinder our success. Conflicting standards and beliefs can significantly impact our ability to focus and achieve our financial goals. Proper focus emerges when we wholeheartedly believe in our path, as our core beliefs empower us to overcome challenges and move steadily toward our objectives. To illustrate this point, let's consider a mountaineer aiming to conquer a peak. If reaching the mountain top is their heartfelt desire, they will remain steadfast on their path, undeterred by adverse weather conditions. However, their focus becomes elusive if their goal is merely influenced by external pressure or expectations. This internal conflict clouds their judgment, and they constantly question the worthiness of risking their life for this endeavour. Negative thoughts and doubts engulf their mind, causing them to magnify the dangers and imagine constant peril. Consequently, the goal of reaching the summit loses its allure, and at the slightest obstacle, they shift their focus to the difficulties and ultimately give up. Sometimes, they might persist halfway through the journey, but internal doubts eventually force them to conform to societal expectations rather than pursue their true aspirations. The lesson is that internal conflicts are formidable adversaries that can drain the motivation and drive needed for success. If conflicting beliefs about wealth coexist, the same pattern of losing focus and succumbing to obstacles may emerge. Our attention shifts from achieving financial prosperity to the perceived difficulties in our path, leading to failure. Like the mountaineer, we might surrender after covering only a portion of the journey towards wealth.

Such internal conflicts create a sense of impending doom, paralysing us from fully committing to our aspirations. Even when external circumstances seem calm, internal turmoil can endanger us, hindering progress. When significant internal conflicts persist, we may attempt to overlook them temporarily, but ultimately, to ensure our immediate well-being, we submit to these doubts and choose paths that promise comfort and safety in the short term. For instance, a person with a weak desire for wealth and a fear of the challenges it may bring will opt for the safe, predictable route, avoiding risks and challenges. The motivation to preserve comfort outweighs the motivation to strive for financial success. To break free from this pattern, resolving inner conflicts and attaining a clear, resolute vision of our financial goals is crucial. By aligning our beliefs and desires, we can regain the power of focus and determination. Acknowledging and addressing our internal doubts allows us to confront external challenges confidently and firmly. Remember, the absence of inner conflict gives us the strength to conquer external obstacles and seize opportunities for financial growth. Therefore, it is vital to introspect and resolve any conflicting beliefs about wealth. Cultivating a genuine desire for prosperity and recognising its worthiness will allow us to steer our focus towards success. By eliminating internal conflicts, we equip ourselves with the mindset necessary to navigate the path to financial achievement with unwavering determination and resilience.

Similarly, a person on a journey towards wealth who holds conflicting beliefs and double standards can be likened to a mountaineer facing a crossroads. Achieving wealth demands effort, determination, and perseverance, while avoiding wealth requires a laid-back and tranquil approach. The exertion and dedication required to amass wealth can wear a person out, and if someone lacks a strong drive for their goal, they might naturally lean towards laziness, unwilling to push forward on the path. Researchers conducted a study involving hundreds of mountaineers ascending a mountain from its base. Along the way, a beautiful shelter was set up where tired climbers could rest. Some mountaineers chose to stay at the shelter and did not continue their journey towards the summit with their friends. They opted for comfort and ease. What intrigued the psychologists was that these individuals looked at their friends who pressed ahead with regret, realising they had chosen comfort over the challenge. However, they could not easily resume their journey after being left behind since their friends had moved ahead. In contrast, those who reached the summit returned to the shelter with pride, while those who stopped midway felt disappointed. Clearly, those who persisted faced challenges and experienced the joy of reaching the summit. On the other hand, those who stayed behind preferred comfort but had conflicting beliefs about their path, ultimately leading to their failure.

To achieve power, wealth, and success, we must adopt the mindset of a motivated mountaineer to reach the summit. Like dedicated Hindu pilgrims, this approach enables us to maintain a high level of focus, helping us overcome all obstacles. Individuals with a strong motivation to achieve a goal naturally possess heightened concentration. They become so engrossed in their objectives that thoughts of difficulties do not easily sway them, and they remain focused. Other factors, such as fear of challenges, do not deter their determination. They inadvertently stay on their path and eventually reach their summit after days or months of persistence. As evident, the difference in mindset and core beliefs in individuals determines whether they triumph over challenges or succumb to them. Those who maintain their focus on the journey hardly notice minor obstacles like snow or rain. They see these experiences as part of the voyage and are prepared to face them. However, those with conflicting beliefs tend to magnify the smallest hindrances, which impede their progress. Therefore, before embarking on the journey towards wealth, it is vital to ask yourself if becoming wealthy is truly your ultimate goal. There are three possible answers: 1) I am doubtful, 2) No, 3) Yes.

If you have doubts, it means a conflicting voice within you needs to be silenced. If you respond with a firm "No," you possess a contented and spiritually-minded disposition, content with the bare minimum. If the answer is "Yes," you have already started your journey towards becoming wealthy. This question was not asked of Donald Trump's brother before he passed away, and the different desires between the two brothers can be attributed to their contrasting central beliefs. Donald Trump's brother was drawn towards addiction, representing a need-seeking individual, often considered short-sighted. He lacked a drive for wealth; even if he possessed it, he was not inclined to strive for more incredible wealth. Pursuing power and wealth was tiresome and tedious as he focused more on present pleasures. On the other hand, individuals like Donald Trump find pleasure in continuous effort and derive satisfaction from tireless striving. He has frequently mentioned in interviews and books about his hard work, waking up early, working until late at night, and even having meals while working.

Embracing a lifestyle geared towards wealth attainment may appear absurd to those prioritising immediate needs and comforts. Understanding your true desires and self-identity becomes crucial in this pursuit. Take a moment to honestly reflect on whether becoming wealthy is your deep-rooted aspiration. If your answer is a resounding "Yes," rest assured that your life is already set on achieving wealth. The power of your determination and focus will pave the way. Imagine the tale of Trump's brother, representing those who prioritise instant gratification, finding themselves stuck at the base camp while their friends progress towards the summit. Regret fills their hearts, but they lack the strength and willpower to leave their sheltered spot and continue the journey. These individuals grapple with conflicting desires, seeking immediate comfort and ambitious goals, which often prove incompatible. Trump's brother, indulging consistently in comfort, couldn't safeguard his wealth, let alone grow it. He faced a crucial choice between perpetual indulgence and pursuing a goal that demanded effort, perseverance, and unwavering determination. Ultimately, he opted for the former, sacrificing his life's potential.

However, you hold the power to redefine your mindset towards wealth and success. By reprogramming your thoughts, you can pave your path to prosperity. Write down this empowering affirmation on paper and make it a daily reminder to keep you focused and determined on your journey. With the right mindset and dedication, you can strive for and achieve the wealth you desire.

> *"I possess a strong inclination towards attaining wealth and prosperity."*

Believe in abundance

The lack of belief in abundance confines us to mental poverty. How can someone envision wealth if they do not believe in abundance? Thus, we must reprogram our minds in this context and correct the belief in scarcity. As human beings, our perspectives are limited. In bustling cities like London, with its vast population, we often only see the walls around us as we leave our homes. The urban lifestyle has constrained us, and our brains have shrunk due to living in smaller spaces. We have become overly cautious and fearful, surrounded by walls, blind to the abundance of resources in the world. In contrast, nomads living in the wilderness understand the vastness and beauty of the world, viewing Earth as their generous mother, providing for their needs without greed.

Although the Earth's abundance remains, inhibiting factors prevent many from living in abundance in the modern era. Excessive greed among a small percentage of the population and a lack of self-confidence among the majority hinder widespread prosperity. They will not become rich until people open their eyes to the Earth's abundance and believe in their capability to acquire wealth. Our beliefs play a vital role in abundance. Positive psychologists advocate mental visualisation to transform our lives, where there are no limitations. By embracing abundance instead of negative emotions, we can experience positive feelings like joy and hope. While our discussion focuses on material abundance, it is also crucial to recognise it in mental, emotional, relational, and spiritual aspects. Believing in abundance enhances one's luck, as luck favours those with unwavering faith in abundance. On the contrary, those lacking such belief may settle for small achievements, preventing them from experiencing miracles and luck. The concept of abundance is deeply connected to our beliefs. Changing our thoughts about wealth is the first step, leading to positive life transformations. Embracing abundance and faith can open doors to opportunities and prosperity in various aspects of life.

Many people do not consider themselves deserving of more because they believe that global resources are limited, and only a select few are deemed worthy enough to benefit from them. Among those who do see themselves as deserving, some selfishly take disproportionately large shares of resources for themselves. Now, shifting the focus to Donald Trump's life, besides mentioning his intelligence and opportunism, let's examine his and his father's life from another perspective. Trump's father built affordable homes for average and poor individuals who were content with paying rent and energy bills. However, he accumulated immense wealth by exploiting the rights of ordinary people from middle and lower-class backgrounds. His contracts with the Manhattan municipality granted him special privileges for housing construction, enabling him to amass wealth day by day. He enjoyed benefits that were out of reach for thousands of others. Despite municipalities being funded by people's taxes, only a small portion of the population had access to the benefits Trump's father enjoyed. This was because they had meticulously planned and schemed, engaging with the right individuals based on their mental images and capturing their ultimate attention. Essentially, they had a blueprint and program to obtain these privileges. While they lacked significant financial power initially, they held strong beliefs in abundance, and luck seemed to favour them.

In this work, I will explore the ethical orientation of individual behaviour and actions without taking a stance on whether these behaviours are right or wrong. The primary focus of this book is not to judge the correctness or incorrectness of someone's conduct; instead, I aim to illustrate the acquisition of power. I will not delve into how specific individuals may have gained power through questionable means, as that is beyond the scope of this book.

Do you attract wealth or poverty?

Humans are naturally drawn to whatever captures their attention. When people lack confidence, they focus on their perceived shortcomings, making attracting abundance into their lives challenging. To shed more light on this concept, let's explore a psychological experiment known as the "selective attention theory."

According to this theory, our surroundings are filled with overwhelming sensory information. Naturally, our brains can't process all of it simultaneously. This is where selective attention steps in. It is our brain's remarkable ability to zoom in on specific details while disregarding irrelevant or distracting information. Selective attention simplifies our lives by enabling us to concentrate on what matters at any given moment while temporarily filtering out the noise. We employ this phenomenon daily, whether focusing on news feeds on our smartphones amidst a crowded metro, having a conversation with a friend in a bustling café, or, in this case, reading this article and paying attention to every word as we go along. To demonstrate the power of selective attention, a captivating experiment was conducted by **Daniel Simons** and **Christopher Chabris**. They asked volunteers to watch a 60-second video of students playing basketball and instructed them to count the number of passes made. However, something surprising happened during the video. About halfway through, a person dressed in a gorilla suit calmly walked into the centre of the frame, thumped her chest like a gorilla, and then nonchalantly left. Astonishingly, almost half of the volunteers failed to notice the gorilla amidst their focus on counting passes. This experiment exemplifies how selective attention can make us oblivious to unexpected but significant environmental elements when our minds are preoccupied with specific tasks. It reinforces the idea that what we pay attention to shapes our perception of the world around us. Similarly, if we constantly focus on our deficiencies and lack confidence, we may overlook opportunities and abundance that could be right in front of us. Hence, cultivating a positive and confident mindset can be pivotal in attracting more favourable outcomes into our lives.

Why did this happen? It's very simple. Because people focused on the ball, they didn't even notice the gorilla on the basketball court. Experiments demonstrate that we overlook other things when we concentrate on one subject. If we excessively focus on shortages, we won't perceive abundance. A documentary filmmaker travelled to Africa and found a region where children didn't even have shoes. The filmmaker wanted to capture their dreams and showcase them to the world. Surprisingly, their wishes were very modest. One child desired shoes, while another wished for a warm meal. These individuals grew up in an environment of scarcity, unable to see abundance. If they don't recognise abundance, the universe won't offer them more than a pair of shoes and a warm meal. To attract greater power, we must fix our gaze on that power. We must believe in abundance for it to open doors of wealth for us. When we truly believe in abundance, luck will come our way.

In capitalist societies, all efforts have been made to present resources as limited. Whenever individuals attain sufficient income and wealth, governments create or reveal an economic problem and a crisis to push people back towards scarcity-oriented thinking. On the other hand, extensive advertising in these societies promotes beautiful goods and luxurious lifestyles, making people constantly strive to obtain them and be content with only acquiring a portion of these possessions. Individuals in capitalist societies are perpetually indebted to banks and major corporations, with some remaining in debt until the end of their lives. Someone who believes in abundance knows that behind every artificially created crisis, a think tank is working to increase their wealth and keep people in fear. Therefore, a person should not be deceived even by media propaganda. If we have faith in abundance, luck will come our way.

Luck means being generously open to existence and having the power of attraction. Pop psychology has heavily emphasised the power of attraction and led many people into a world of illusion. They focus solely on the power of attraction without addressing individual capabilities, the method of seeking and advancing expertise. As a result, these individuals spend their lives thinking about an idea or acquiring something without maintaining ultimate faith in the power of attraction. Although delving into the power of attraction somewhat deviates from our scientific domain, I should elaborate on my reasons scientifically. Through the power of attraction, we can achieve many of our desires, but there are certain conditions that we must adhere to.

If we apply the idea of abundance to **Donald Trump**, his life and career reveal a deep belief in limitless potential and unwavering confidence. Trump's approach to everything—business, politics, and even personal branding—has been rooted in the idea that the world offers endless opportunities for those who dare to seize them. It's as if he thrives on the belief that success is not a finite resource but an ever-flowing river available to anyone bold enough to dip their hands in. Take, for instance, **Trump's Real**

Estate Empire. Initially, he never settled for small projects or modest ambitions. Instead, he reached for the sky—literally. The towering elegance of **Trump Tower** in New York, the opulence of **Mar-a-Lago**, and his ventures into luxury hotels and casinos were all emblematic of a man who believed there was always room for growth. Even in the fiercely competitive world of real estate, Trump seemed to approach every deal with the mindset that success wasn't just possible; it was inevitable.

His philosophy is perhaps most clearly articulated in his bestselling book, **"The Art of the Deal"**. Here, Trump lays bare his approach to life: be bold, take risks, and never fear asking for what you believe you deserve. Opportunities, he asserts, are everywhere. This belief in abundance is at the core of his thinking—success isn't about avoiding failure; it's about seeing potential where others see obstacles. The very act of making deals becomes an art form, a dance where the focus is always on what can be gained, never on what might be lost.

Nowhere was Trump's belief in abundance more visible than during his 2016 presidential campaign. While the political world largely dismissed his chances, he charged forward with unwavering confidence. His now-iconic slogan, "Make America Great Again," wasn't just a political statement; it was a promise of abundance. It was a vision of a prosperous future where opportunity and success were within reach for every American who was willing to embrace it. Even when faced with intense criticism and near-universal doubt, Trump focused on winning, thriving, and creating a future filled with possibilities.

His media presence further amplifies this belief in abundance. From his name emblazoned on skyscrapers to the hit television show **"The Apprentice"**, Trump expanded his brand across industries, constantly reinforcing his idea that success is infinite. His ability to leverage his image and turn it into a multi-faceted empire reflects his conviction that wealth and influence are not confined to any one arena—they are limitless as long as you believe in your ability to create them. And while many may attribute Trump's risks and boldness to his wealth, I believe this misses the mark. What drives him is not his bank account but his mindset—a relentless spirit that refuses to accept limits. One moment from his presidential campaign stands out vividly in my mind. During an event, he was physically attacked, his ear bleeding from the assault. It was a vulnerable moment, but instead of showing weakness, he stood taller, his fist raised high in defiance, shouting "Fight, fight, fight!" That moment wasn't about wealth. It was about his indomitable will, a reflection of a man who sees no scarcity in strength or opportunity, only abundance in everything.

It's easy to misunderstand or criticize such a mindset, especially in a world where scarcity often feels more real than abundance. But I believe people are defined not by their bank accounts but by their belief in what's possible. Trump's life is a testament to that belief—to the power of seeing the world as a place filled with opportunity rather than one marked by limitations.

Let's examine the characteristics of a person who believes in the power of attraction.

Characteristics of optimistic individuals:

Having a clear and accurate view of yourself:

In my practice, I have met countless individuals who longed for clarity but found themselves adrift, lacking a vivid and detailed vision of their future. When I asked them about their goals, their answers were often frustratingly vague, like distant clouds on the horizon—shapeless and hard to grasp. They would say things like, *"I want a good job"* or *"I want my children to live comfortably,"* but without any depth or specificity. Those suffering from anxiety and stress were particularly unclear about what they truly needed, trapped in the fog of uncertainty.

On the other hand, those who had even dipped into the simplest self-help books—yes, even the clichéd ones—seemed to grasp the concept of attraction better. They could articulate their desires with an almost poetic precision. I recall one woman vividly. She came to me, already imagining her future husband in her mind. He wasn't just some vague figure; she had pictured him in fine detail. *"I always see him as a surgeon, working in a hospital,"* she told me. She had even painted his face in her imagination. For two years, she distanced herself from every man she met—whether at work, in shops, or at social gatherings—who didn't match the vision she had so carefully crafted. In her mind, she was already living with this man, as if he were real, as if they had already crossed paths. After she applied the techniques I recommended, she sharpened her focus even further, identifying her abilities and aligning herself with her most profound aspirations. She worked tirelessly towards this vision, never wavering. And yes, as you've probably guessed, she eventually married a surgeon who closely mirrored the man she had envisioned. But was this a miracle? A mere coincidence? In truth, it was both. It was neither a miracle nor coincidence in the traditional sense, but it became one because she used the power of mental visualisation to shape her own destiny.

There is a world of difference between someone who believes in the power of attraction and someone who wishes for things to happen. The former is deliberate and precise, almost like a sculptor chiselling away at a block of marble to reveal their desires. They craft their dreams with intention, formulating plans and strategies, whereas the latter floats through life, hoping for the best without any clarity or direction. Take, for instance, the many single women who came to see me. When asked about the type of partner they envisioned, their answers were often vague and filled with generalities. Rarely did they have a clear mental image of the person they were hoping to meet. But when we delve into the practice of mental visualisation, something extraordinary happens. Does it hold some supernatural power that magically leads us to our goals? Of course not. So, what is it, then?

1. **Mental visualisation directs us toward our goals.** Imagine you are infatuated with a sleek black Mercedes Benz, complete with striking red interior trim. You see it so clearly in your mind that it almost feels real. You begin to notice this car everywhere—on the streets, in car dealerships, and even in conversations with friends. Your focus on this car becomes so sharp that other vehicles fade into the background, and soon, your friends start to associate you with this particular

Mercedes. Eventually, you can see yourself behind the wheel. This is the simplicity of achieving desires through visualisation: focus and concentration lead us closer to what we seek.

2. **Mental visualisation also helps us evaluate how to reach our goals.** Once we create a mental image, we begin to break down the steps needed to achieve it. Returning to the Mercedes Benz example, you might begin investigating its price or exploring financing options. If your budget is lacking, you'll consider saving or taking advantage of instalment plans. Visualisation activates the mind to strategies, pushing us forward towards our aspirations.

3. **Finally, mental visualisation shifts the brain from beta to alpha waves.** But what does this mean? The human brain operates on different frequencies depending on our state of mind. Beta waves, with a frequency range of 13 to 45 Hz, are active when we are fully awake and engaged in daily tasks—working, cooking, and talking. Stress causes the brain to produce higher beta frequencies, while relaxation lowers them. In contrast, alpha waves, with frequencies of 8 to 12 Hz, occur when we close our eyes and relax, remaining aware of our surroundings. It is in this tranquil state, where the brain can't process visual information, that mental imagery thrives. This is where visualisation flourishes, guiding us forward on our life journey.

Through this delicate balance of focus, analysis, and relaxation, we begin to sculpt our future, one mental image at a time. And while it may not be a miracle in the traditional sense, the power of visualisation can feel nothing short of miraculous.

Let me walk you through the idea of buying a **Mercedes-Benz** in a more intimate and accessible way, one that reveals the subtle yet powerful process behind how our minds work when pursuing something seemingly out of reach. Imagine, in the real world, someone visits a dealership and is instantly captivated by the sleek beauty of a Mercedes. They inspect the car and feel the luxury in every detail, but when they glance at the price tag, it's far beyond their budget. A sense of despair may creep in, their heart sinks, and their thoughts spiral into stress. At this moment, their brain's activity surges, and they convince themselves that owning the car is simply impossible. The dream fades, and they return to their everyday life, disheartened.

But here's where things get interesting. Our brain, when in a calm, semi-conscious state – known as the alpha state – tells a different story. In this deeply relaxed mental state, brainwaves slow down, and the barriers between what we think is possible and impossible blur. Visualisation becomes more potent, and suddenly, the idea of owning that **Mercedes-Benz** feels less like a distant fantasy and more like a genuine possibility. In the alpha state, we begin to focus with remarkable clarity. This is the state where learning, problem-solving, and creative thinking flourish. In fact, visualisation in this state bridges the gap between the real world and the imaginary, opening the door to solutions that seemed unattainable moments before.

Let me take you through the technique of visualisation, seamlessly paired with the practice of entering the alpha state. While this book doesn't delve deeply into the method itself, it provides a simple way to achieve this state and harness its power. Imagine yourself lying comfortably, eyes closed, gazing upwards towards the ceiling. Without moving, start counting backwards. Alternatively, light a candle and focus on the flickering flame, allowing your brainwaves to slow, gently guiding you into the alpha state. Over time, as you repeat this process, you'll count down from one hundred to one, then reduce it to fifty, and eventually, to just five. With practice, reaching this state becomes natural and effortless. Once in the alpha state, visualisation begins. Picture yourself in the driver's seat of that **Mercedes-Benz**, cruising down an open road with the sun on your face and the steering wheel beneath your hands. This isn't just daydreaming; it's a powerful mental image that influences your brain in profound ways. Psychologists have long discovered that mental imagery when linked with the alpha state, can bring about extraordinary outcomes. Your brain, one of the most complex entities in existence, starts to align your reality with this vision.

After visualising your goal, you return to your everyday life, and your brain is now back in its active, problem-solving beta state. However, something has shifted. You move with more confidence and positivity towards your goal, inspired by the image you've planted in your mind. This process is not a new phenomenon. Every great invention, every breakthrough, was once merely an image in someone's mind. Consider the mobile phone. Fifty years ago, if someone had told you that you could talk face-to-face with people across the world through small screens, it would have sounded like science fiction. Yet, the inventors of this technology visualised the concept long before it became a reality. They turned their mental imagery into a tangible product, and now, we use it every day. However, there are those who may say they've visualised their goals for years, yet nothing has come of it. So, what holds them back? Why do some achieve success while others don't, despite practising mental visualisation?

Through careful observation, two key types of people emerge. The first are those who don't maintain a continuous and focused mental image (Group A). They allow their vision to waver, and without that steady image, it's difficult for the mind to anchor to the goal. The second group includes those who don't believe in the power of their own visualisation (Group B). Without faith in the process, even the clearest mental image won't manifest into reality. Understanding these distinctions sheds light on why visualisation works for some and not for others – it's a delicate balance of clarity, persistence, and belief. Ultimately, this journey begins in the mind, where imagination, guided by practice and belief, becomes the blueprint for our reality.

A: Individuals Who Lack Continuous Mental Imagery

The first category of individuals comprises those who, while harbouring hopes and dreams, have yet to fully embrace the true power of mental imagery. They lead lives of quiet routine, occasionally allowing their minds to wander toward their goals, but these moments are fleeting, like fragile wisps of thought that quickly dissolve into the noise of daily life. Their daydreams are delicate, ephemeral, and soon forgotten. Their approach has a certain hesitance, as though they only half-believe in the magic of their own imagination. For these individuals, the connection between their inner world and their outer actions remains tentative, creating an almost imperceptible contradiction between what they long for and what they actively pursue. The lack of consistent mental engagement weakens the potency of their aspirations, as though their desires float unanchored in a sea of distractions. Their internal dialogue meanders, uncertain, and fails to offer the strength needed to propel them forward. To truly harness the power of mental imagery, individuals in this category must adopt a more devoted practice— one of intentional reflection and mindfulness. By understanding the profound value of this inner vision, they can weave together their thoughts and actions into a seamless tapestry, creating a force that drives them toward their dreams. With dedication, their internal dialogue will no longer be a faint whisper but a resounding voice of clarity, aligning perfectly with their external journey.

B: Individuals Who Lack Belief in Positive Visualization

The second category consists of those who may dabble in the practice of mental imagery but need more deep-rooted conviction to unlock its true potential. They might stumble upon the concept of positive visualisation through social media or casual conversations, but their belief in its transformative power remains half-hearted at best. This hesitation becomes a barrier, preventing them from fully embracing the process. After a few unsuccessful attempts, they often grow disheartened, dismissing the exercise as a whimsical notion rather than a powerful tool for change. Some even ridicule themselves, feeling foolish for engaging in what they perceive as an empty ritual. Yet, to truly harness the power of visualisation, one must nurture an unshakeable belief in its ability to bring about meaningful change. It is not a fleeting trend or a shallow pastime—it is a deeply personal and powerful process that can reshape one's reality. For those in this category, the journey begins with cultivating faith in its effectiveness. Doubts must be set aside and replaced by unwavering trust in the process. With this shift in mindset, mental imagery can become a profound force in their lives, allowing them to transcend limitations and realise their full potential. When visualisation is approached with sincerity and dedication, it ceases to be a mere mental exercise and transforms into a life-altering practice. The results are not instantaneous but unfold over time, as belief and consistency feed the imagination and bring about real, tangible change. By engaging regularly with heartfelt visualisation, individuals invite clarity, focus, and inner strength into their lives, ensuring a balanced and effective mental landscape. In prioritising and believing in the power of mental imagery, they allow themselves to be truly present in its transformative space, unlocking its profound possibilities.

There are countless inspiring stories of individuals who have harnessed the power of visualisation to transform their lives. These stories remind us that visualisation can bring remarkable results when combined with belief and determination.

Jim Carrey is one such example. In the early days of his career, long before he became a household name, Carrey struggled to succeed. At a particularly difficult time in the early 1990s, he wrote himself a cheque for ten million dollars, payable for "acting services rendered," and dated it for Thanksgiving a few years into the future. He kept this cheque in his wallet, visualising daily the success and opportunity he desired. By 1994, with his breakout role in *Dumb and Dumber*, Carrey's vision had become a reality, as he earned the exact sum he had written. His story is a testament to how visualisation, paired with unwavering belief, can create extraordinary outcomes.

Oprah Winfrey, one of the world's most influential media figures, has long advocated the power of visualisation. Oprah openly shares her practice of creating vision boards—a tool where she carefully selects images and words that represent her dreams and goals. From owning her own network to building her media empire, she credits this method with helping to manifest many of her life's ambitions. Oprah's mantra, "You become what you believe," underscores her deep conviction in the transformative power of visualisation and focused intention.

Similarly, **Arnold Schwarzenegger** embraced visualisation while becoming a bodybuilding legend. Before he became a Hollywood star or governor of California, Schwarzenegger would mentally rehearse his bodybuilding performances, picturing himself winning competitions and sculpting the perfect physique. He visualised every detail: the poses, the crowd's reactions, and the overwhelming sense of victory. His dedication to this practice led him to become a seven-time Mr Olympia, opening doors to a thriving career in both film and politics.

The legendary Olympic swimmer **Michael Phelps** also turned to visualisation as a key part of his training regimen. From a young age, Phelps would visualise every stroke of his race, every challenge he might face, and how he would ultimately emerge victorious. This mental rehearsal was so thorough that it included scenarios such as his goggles filling with water, which actually occurred during one of his Olympic races. Visualizing the victories and potential setbacks allowed him to remain calm and composed under pressure, paving the way for his unparalleled record of 23 gold medals.

Sarah Blakely, the visionary founder of Spanx, attributes much of her success to visualisation. Before launching her now globally successful brand, Blakely would visualise herself on *The Oprah Winfrey Show*, receiving Oprah's coveted endorsement. This vision became a reality, catapulting Spanx into the global spotlight and establishing Blakely as a self-made billionaire. Her story is one of persistence, belief, and the power of maintaining a clear vision, even in the face of initial rejections.

In the world of mixed martial arts, **Conor McGregor** is another figure who has spoken extensively about the role of visualisation in his success. Before his meteoric rise in the UFC, McGregor would repeatedly visualise himself winning fights, predicting how his victories would unfold. He would imagine the arenas, the crowd, and the moment he knocked out his opponents. This practice, combined with his relentless hard work, helped him rise to become a two-division UFC champion and one of the sport's most recognisable names.

Our case study, **Donald Trump**, offers a striking example of how the power of visualisation can be used to shape not only business ventures but entire careers. Throughout his life, Trump has been a firm advocate for the art of positive thinking and, perhaps more crucially, the ability to see success in the mind's eye long before it materialises in the physical world. This unwavering belief in the power of visualisation has been a driving force behind many of his most daring achievements. In his 1987 book, **"The Art of the Deal,"** Trump reveals the depth of his conviction in thinking big and visualising triumphant outcomes. His approach was not mere daydreaming but a focused, deliberate method of manifesting success. Whether it was the transformation of the **Grand Hyatt Hotel** in New York or the creation of the iconic **Trump Tower**, his ability to envision the end result well before the first brick was laid became a cornerstone of his business strategy. Trump saw not just the empty buildings or rundown spaces in front of him but the glittering potential that lay beyond—he imagined the grandeur, the success, the acclaim. This practice of visualisation was wider than his business life. When Trump turned his gaze to politics, particularly during his 2016 presidential campaign, he once again used visualisation as a tool. Long before the votes were cast, Trump envisioned himself as President of the United States. The slogan **"Make America Great Again"** was more than just a phrase; it was a vision he repeatedly projected, both to his supporters and to himself. He painted a picture of a revitalised America, positioning himself as the leader who could bring that vision to life. His ability to visualise his success, coupled with an unshakeable confidence, became a self-fulfilling prophecy, helping to propel him to the highest office in the land.

Trump's journey demonstrates how visualisation, when paired with relentless confidence and action, can transcend the boundaries of mere ambition. His belief in thinking positively, seeing success before it happens, and projecting unwavering confidence forms the essence of his method for achieving his goals. It's this mindset that has guided him from bold real estate ventures to the very pinnacle of political power.

These powerful stories illustrate that visualisation is far more than daydreaming; it is a deeply personal and transformative practice. These individuals turned their dreams into reality by focusing their minds on their desired outcomes and wholeheartedly believing in their visions. Visualisation, when practised with conviction, can open doors, reveal possibilities, and lead to extraordinary success.

2. Individuals who believe in the power of favourable attraction tend to be optimistic.

While they may sometimes come across as dreamy or excessively optimistic, there lies a profound belief within them in the superhuman force of attraction. This conviction shapes their outlook, allowing them to perceive the world through a lens tinted with hope and positivity, often outshining those around them. Though they may face derision from friends and acquaintances, they pay little heed to such opinions;

their unwavering faith serves as a beacon, illuminating the path to their growth.

Consider two individuals, both harbouring the dream of homeownership yet lacking the necessary funds. One, infused with an enduring belief in the power of attraction, remains resolutely optimistic. The other, however, finds themselves ensnared in a web of doubt. As the optimistic dreamer consistently saves, they envision each coin as a stepping stone, drawing ever closer to their goal. In stark contrast, the other individual fixates on the emptiness of their glass, becoming increasingly despondent as the chasm between their aspirations and reality widens. This essential difference in mindset manifests in profound ways. The one who embraces the power of attraction cultivates positive thoughts, fostering uplifting emotions that propel them forward. Their heart brims with enthusiasm, determination, and an indomitable hope that guides their actions. Meanwhile, negative thoughts imprison the other, drawing attention solely to their current possessions. This lack of belief sows discontent, leading to a habit of finding fault in their modest belongings. In turn, this negativity breeds a cycle of disappointment that shapes their behaviour, compelling them to squander their limited resources on trivial pursuits or fleeting distractions.

Fast forward a decade, and the contrast is stark: the optimistic individual, buoyed by their belief, has methodically saved enough to make a down payment and has transitioned from a tenant to a proud homeowner. In essence, their journey encapsulates the principles of Cognitive Behavioural Therapy (CBT), which underscores the interplay between belief and behaviour.

Through the lens of CBT, we can unravel the profound impact of these beliefs on behaviour:

Positive Thoughts: The believer in attraction nurtures optimistic musings, allowing them to envision success and hone in on opportunities for saving and investing.

Positive Emotions: Such uplifting thoughts naturally breed emotions that inspire action, filling them with a sense of determination and hope.

Effective Behaviour: Guided by these positive feelings, they engage in prudent financial choices, wisely allocating resources that inch them closer to their dream.

Success: This harmonious cycle of positive thoughts, emotions, and actions ultimately culminates in tangible success. The individual who believes in the power of attraction finds themselves empowered and ready to make that long-awaited down payment.

Conversely, the individual steeped in negativity follows a disheartening trajectory:

Negative Thoughts: Doubts and pessimism cloud their mind, fixating on what they lack and fostering a crippling sense of inadequacy.

Negative Emotions: These thoughts naturally spiral into negative emotions—despondency, disappointment, and resignation—that weigh heavily upon their spirit.

Ineffective Behaviour: Overwhelmed by these emotions, they engage in self-sabotaging behaviours, squandering meagre savings on low-value purchases or unnecessary expenses, further entrenching their distance from their goal.

Lack of Success: Trapped in this cycle of negativity, they remain tenants, seemingly forever stuck, with no significant progress toward the dream of homeownership.

In essence, the belief in the power of attraction is not merely a whimsical notion; it is a transformative force that can shape destinies and guide individuals toward the lives they aspire to lead.

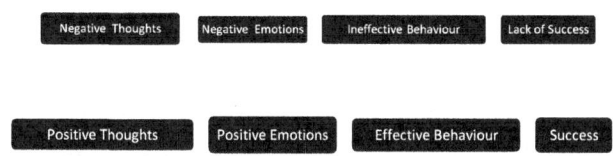

So, we have discussed two groups: one that always focuses on deficiencies and either does not perceive abundance or refuses to acknowledge it, and another group that firmly believes in abundance. The latter group consistently achieves their goals, especially material ones. Now, let's focus on analysing the personality of the first group and how they can bring about personal changes.

Characteristics of pessimistic individuals:

1. Low self-esteem:

They believe they are financially inadequate in all aspects of life. They think they are not sufficiently beautiful, intelligent, kind, talented, hardworking, attractive, or lovable. This core belief imposes a sense of unworthiness upon them, leading them to believe they do not deserve the best due to their inadequacy. Low self-esteem is like a prison in which the person is trapped and doesn't even consider themselves worthy of being freed. Therefore, the first step is to change this core belief and learn to love oneself. Such individuals may not even recognise their own abundance despite having numerous qualities. Thus, the initial change should occur in their beliefs.

Donald Trump is not afflicted by self-centeredness, but he loves himself. Despite people, especially TV presenters or comedians, mocking his way of speaking or hairstyle, Trump refers to his hair as "famous hair." He has confidence in his appearance, which gives him high self-esteem, enabling him to engage in significant and challenging endeavours. Therefore, to believe in abundance, we must first believe in ourselves. We should even accept our flaws and transform them into strengths. By loving ourselves and having faith in our abilities, we take the first step towards embracing abundance.

"Love yourself first, and everything else falls into line. You have to love yourself to get anything done in this world." - Lucille Ball

2. Lack of self-efficacy:

Everything stems from the belief of inadequacy. When a person feels inadequate, they naturally lack a positive sense of self-efficacy. Individuals not embracing abundance also look down upon their possessions and capabilities. They fail to properly assess their abilities and tend to give up quickly when faced with challenges instead of utilising their talents and capabilities. Their worldview and self-awareness have a direct impact on each other. Just as they fail to see abundance in the world, they consider their talents and abilities insignificant. Consequently, they surrender quickly to even the slightest problems and seek refuge in isolation.

Self-efficacy, the belief in one's ability to accomplish tasks and achieve goals, was first elaborated in detail by one of the greatest Canadian psychologists, **Albert Bandura**. He initiated the "Social Learning Theory," later known as the "Social Cognitive Theory." According to him, individuals learn self-efficacy from family and society. If someone lacks a deep sense of self-efficacy, they must reconsider their core beliefs.

Have you ever thought about the changes in a person after re-evaluating their core beliefs and achieving a deep sense of self-efficacy? I will briefly mention a few:

- They believe they have what it takes to accomplish a task.
- They believe they possess the skills and capabilities required for change.
- They believe they can and should reach their goals, which require time, planning, and effort.
- They believe they can, too, if someone else can do it.
- They believe they can achieve the seemingly impossible through effort, learning, and action.

After these remarkable changes, the individual's ideology and worldview will also alter, and they will genuinely embrace abundance. However, one may still encounter failure despite self-confidence and a strong sense of self-efficacy. Accepting that failure is a part of the success process is crucial. Albert Bandura states, "Self-efficacy does not necessarily guarantee success, but lack of self-efficacy assuredly leads to failure."

3. Choosing self-destructive instead of self-empowerment

Those who lack belief in managing their emotions have little control over their emotional choices. They tend to focus more on the feelings and desires of others rather than their own. Furthermore, they opt for an external perspective rather than introspecting, constantly reviewing themselves from the viewpoint of others. This tactical mistake perpetuates feelings of inadequacy, which remain persistent and alive in them.

When we view ourselves through the lens of others, we will always find weaknesses and problems. Everyone has their own standards for life, and trying to conform to others' standards is futile. For instance, if our neighbour's standard is to turn off the lights at 9 PM, and we prefer staying awake until 11 PM, trying to match our neighbour's preference will leave us dissatisfied. Similarly, if our co-worker's standard is to be thin and our weight is slightly higher, we will feel ashamed in their presence. Hundreds of other examples can be added, but one must not forget that we are unique individuals with different beliefs, needs, and desires. Instead of looking outside ourselves, we must introspect and ask, "Who am I, and what do I want from life?"

Individuals who constantly scrutinise themselves through others' lenses engage in mental self-flagellation, always seeking signs of their weaknesses.

Let me provide an example. Suppose you are married with two children possess relative beauty, and are in a relatively good financial situation. You are invited to a party. Instead of enjoying your assets and spending time in pleasure, you engage in comparing yourself to others. In this gathering, someone may surpass you in beauty, another may have a better job, another might have successful children, and one of the guests' husbands may be wealthier than yours. This cycle continues, and you perceive yourself through a lens of deficiency. Most likely, other guests are doing the same, engaging in self-comparisons. All these comparisons lead to self-destruction. Nevertheless, this person unconsciously strives to present a facade that conceals their vulnerabilities. For example, they try to appear more beautiful through heavy makeup or pressure their spouse to buy an expensive car. Yet, despite all these efforts, the sense of self-destruction remains. In reality, these individuals resemble puppets controlled by others, and others' opinions shape their emotions and desires. Here is where one must ponder. They must cultivate abundant faith and realise their assets are incomparable to others. Then, with unwavering faith, they should map their future.

4. In the perspective of these individuals, deficiencies outweigh abundance.

From the perspective of some individuals, deficiencies tend to outweigh abundance. However, it's fascinating to understand how those with abundant beliefs perceive limitations differently. Instead of getting bogged down by their constraints, they actively seek opportunities and focus on abundance in life. It's essential to acknowledge that limitations are a natural aspect of our existence. For example, humans lack the innate ability to fly like birds. Nonetheless, the power of abundance allows us to overcome these limitations in remarkable ways. Consider this: despite being unable to fly like birds, humans have invented aeroplanes that carry hundreds of people soaring high in the sky. If people were to concentrate on their limitations and accept them as insurmountable solely, we would have never witnessed the wonders of aviation or set foot on the moon.

An insightful example comes from Donald Trump's book "Never Give Up." Trump shares how he has faced numerous failures in deals throughout his career. However, these setbacks never caused him to lose faith in himself or in abundance. Instead, he approached these challenges differently, leveraging his creativity to restart his endeavours and ultimately achieve success. Rather than being limited by failure, his resilience and innovative thinking propelled him beyond his competitors.

The key takeaway is that a mindset of abundance can shift our perspective on limitations. Rather than allowing constraints to restrict us, embracing abundance empowers us to find creative solutions, exceed expectations, and manifest success. By recognising that limitations are a part of life, yet abundance holds the potential to transcend them, we open ourselves to a world of endless possibilities and accomplishments. So, let's adopt an outlook of abundance and witness how it can unlock new avenues of growth and achievement in our lives.

5. Individuals needing more belief in abundance have shaky beliefs.

This principle must always be kept in mind and repeatedly emphasised. It is belief in success. If someone has shaky beliefs, they will not come close to the doors of success. Those who believe in abundance become addicted to positive beliefs. They create mantras to reinforce their minds with the belief in abundance. Mantras that abundance believers adhere to include:

- "I am abundant."
- "I am wealthy."
- "I am enough."
- "I am extraordinary."
- "I am happy."

These affirmations are used to reinforce their belief in abundance.

Repeating these mantras should become a habit. Even in the most challenging situations, one should repeat these positive mantras and condition them to their circumstances. Even when facing a significant tragedy, these mantras should be repeated to establish them in the mind firmly. Such an individual will always live in their own mental paradise.

While reading the book, review your mind. Are you among those who repeat positive mantras, feel content with what they have, and express gratitude? Or do you constantly complain and protest? If you are the type who continually focuses on your weaknesses, be aware that you lack abundance. You have empowered your weaknesses to define your entire being. Your existence has been filled with weaknesses, and you no longer see the power to change within yourself. If you are the type who constantly complains and glorifies their misfortunes, you must change your perspective. If your belief is in misfortune, then why should good fortune come your way? The great German philosopher Friedrich Nietzsche has a very accurate interpretation. He says, "He who fights with monsters should be careful lest he thereby become a monster. And if you gaze long into an abyss, the abyss will also gaze into you." In other words, if you believe and have faith in your incompetence, inadequacy, and unworthiness for a long time, these attributes will become a reality, and you will become a person who is unfit, incapable, and weak. Therefore, wash your eyes and look at yourself and your life differently. Repeat your mantras every day until you deeply believe in them.

6. The confidence of these individuals is fragile.

The confidence of individuals can be fragile, but it is crucial to recognise and embrace our inherent imperfections. Like all beings, humans are not perfect, yet they can still be sufficient with these imperfections. True self-confidence comes from acknowledging that we can achieve our desires in the physical world despite our limitations and vulnerabilities. This belief is at the core of successful individuals' mindsets. It is essential to understand that limitations are an inherent aspect of existence. From rocks to rivers to seas, every form of existence experiences its own set of limitations. Once we accept this reality, we can explore the power we hold to overcome some of these constraints. Confident individuals approach life as a battlefield against limitations, taking on challenges with determination and resolve. In contrast, those lacking confidence tend to surrender to these limitations without putting up a fight. Take the example of the inevitability of death. While it is true that death is an unavoidable aspect of life, confident individuals throughout history have fought against it. Medical science and surgery advancements are a testament to the human determination to overcome the obstacles presented by illnesses and extend life. Confident individuals believe in their talents and abilities, knowing they can find solutions even in the most challenging circumstances. On the other hand, someone lacking confidence tends to focus on their limitations, leading them to give up quickly in the face of obstacles.

If you have yet to achieve the desired success, it might be worth examining whether you have surrendered too quickly. Even the most minor failures can often lead to feelings of surrender and defeat. The key is to say "no" to surrender and instead reassess your approach to life. Embrace your imperfections, acknowledge your abilities, and remain determined to keep going despite challenges. With renewed confidence and a refusal to give up, you can redefine the trajectory of your life. Remember that self-confidence is not about being perfect but believing in your capacity to navigate life's ups and downs with resilience and courage.

7. *These individuals are miserly.*

You must be surprised. Those who lack belief in abundance try to hoard their acquired wealth and fear giving it away. However, religious individuals have faith in abundance in the afterlife, which leads them to be deceived by charlatans. These charlatans are religious leaders who promise abundant rewards in the next world by instilling fear in their followers and demanding money to attain that abundance. Hence, religious individuals perceive generosity as a means of gaining access to abundance in the afterlife. But this mindset is detrimental. Someone who believes in abundance in this world gives without hesitation, knowing that this act of giving will attract more abundance, and they will indeed have greater access to it. These individuals consistently give everything: kindness, compassion, time, empathy, and money. **Laozi** says, "When you realise nothing is lacking, the whole world belongs to you." The difference between someone who believes in abundance and someone who lacks belief lies in the former's understanding of giving as a means of receiving more, while the latter perceives giving as loss. However, understand my point. I do not suggest that one should give away all their possessions recklessly. Those who believe in abundance do not give without consideration. Before giving, they make sure they have enough. They understand that depleting their spiritual, physical, emotional, and financial accounts will not benefit anyone. Thus, they first nurture their source of abundance and then give in a state of tranquillity.

8- Individuals with a belief in scarcity experience various cognitive distortions

What are cognitive distortions? We need cognition to live our lives. We all believe that our cognitions are accurate and correct, but psychologists have demonstrated through numerous experiments that most of us have distorted cognitions about events, our behaviours, and others. Cognitive distortions are internal mental filters or biases that increase our misery, trap us in anxiety, and make us feel bad about ourselves. For instance, suppose today you see your boss angrily entering the office and ignoring you. You might fall into a cognitive distortion and attribute his anger to something related to you. However, if you remain patient, you will discover he is upset about something else. Even if he gets angry with you, you should not get upset. Sometimes, we catastrophise due to cognitive distortions. If he gets angry, we might generalise it to mean he does not like us and will fire us. Put, cognitive distortions can consume your mind and render your behaviour ineffective. These individuals view the world narrowly and perceive limitations in everything. Therefore, their central beliefs are shaped by cognitive distortions. Let me refer to some of their mistaken beliefs rooted in cognitive distortions, and you can add more of your own:

1. Money is not an honest means of acquiring wealth.
2. Wealth is dirty.
3. The wealthy are immoral and unjust.
4. Being wealthy means taking away the rights of others.
5. Abundance is reserved for those born into wealthy families.
6. Success is impossible.
7. I feel anxious, and it's someone else's fault that I am unsuccessful.
8. regardless of what I do or attempt, I can never be happy.
9. If I receive more, others will experience scarcity.

The critical point is to replace limiting beliefs with new beliefs that speak of abundance, not scarcity or deficiency. What are your beliefs regarding wealth and abundance? Write them down for yourself to discover and correct any cognitive distortions. Which of the above sentences do you find yourself repeating? Where did this belief originate from?

9- *They lack enthusiasm for learning or change.*

Individuals who lack a belief in abundance often have limited expertise. Even if they achieve high levels of education, they shy away from acquiring new experiences. They behave like robots, not interested in learning new subjects or changing lives. They are either content with what they have or feel discouraged about fulfilling their desires. On the other hand, those who believe in abundance are satisfied with their possessions, but their contentment stems from their knowledge of abundance. They understand that they live in an abundant world, and their spiritual and material possessions are just a tiny part of that abundance. As a result, these individuals are neither disheartened by not having more nor fearful of losing what they have. They are content with their possessions but recognise their ability to acquire and attract more. Contrarily, those who oppose them, even if content with their possessions, lack a belief in abundance due to a fear of scarcity. These individuals strive harder to obtain and attract more because they believe in the scarcity of resources. They tend to be anxious, unfair, and self-centred. Since they lack confidence in acquiring abundance, they become fixated on previous acquisitions and pursue increasing wealth only through the same means. Even if they become billionaires, they will still not embrace the concept of abundance.

We must review our core beliefs and rectify ineffective ones to alter our mental structure and move towards a successful life. To achieve this, we must have a thorough understanding of ourselves. By completing the table below, you can gain a relatively accurate understanding of your psychological personality.

10- They do not lead an ethical life

Many individuals who lack a belief in abundance often experience a constant sense of anxiety about losing out in life. They perceive that existence is limited, and they fear that if they do not actively acquire resources or share them with others, they will face inevitable losses. As a result, they adopt a selfish mindset, striving to accumulate resources for themselves through various means. In this pursuit, they may disregard the rights of others, feel dissatisfied with putting in an honest effort at work, or resort to deception and lies to amass wealth and possessions. Their actions are driven by deep-seated fears of missing out or not gaining enough, leading them to use any available means to access what they believe are scarce resources.

To better understand which category we belong to, we must reflect on our approach to attracting wealth or any other form of power in our lives. Are we leading an ethical life, mindful of the well-being of others, or have we fallen into the trap of scarcity mentality, driven by fear and self-centeredness? Assessing our values and actions is crucial to ensure we contribute positively to our lives and those around us. By adopting a mindset of abundance, we can foster a more generous and compassionate outlook, creating a positive ripple effect in our communities and beyond.

What is my mental image?	With what tools do I analyse my mental image?	Do I look at myself from the eyes of others or myself?	Do I believe in scarcity or abundance?	What are the signs that I love myself?	Am I stingy in any field?	What are my cognitive distortions?	Am I eager to learn more?

You might be wondering why I listed only two characteristics of optimistic individuals while providing ten characteristics of pessimistic individuals. This disparity highlights an important point: adopting an optimistic outlook requires less energy and effort than maintaining a pessimistic mindset.

Chapter Summary

In the first chapter, we explored the concept of inherent abilities and how everyone possesses the power to achieve their desires. In this chapter, we delved into another crucial aspect: the power of "wanting" and the role of beliefs in shaping our actions. Having great human potential is not enough if we fail to take action towards our goals. "Wanting" is deeply rooted in our beliefs; sometimes, we may not even know how to ask effectively. However, asking is closely linked to cultivating an abundance mindset.

Imagine driving alone on an abandoned desert road, and suddenly, your car breaks down. You realise there's no mobile phone reception as you leave your vehicle. In such a deserted place, with minimal chances of another car passing by, asking for help from a mechanic might not seem rational. The reason behind this reluctance is that you lack the belief in finding assistance in that remote location, and as a result, the act of "wanting" doesn't even take shape. Therefore, the first essential step towards effective asking is wholeheartedly embracing the concept of abundance. You must genuinely believe in your capacity to ask for what you need.

If you desire wealth, it's crucial to understand that the resources and wealth available are infinite. Embracing this abundance mindset will empower you to ask for what you seek. Though it may seem like a simple concept, unfortunately, many people are akin to that stranded driver in the desert who lacks this belief. They tend to focus on their deficiencies, and as a result, they deprive themselves of the power to achieve their wishes. Embracing abundance transforms the act of asking from mere wishful thinking to a powerful force that brings desires into manifestation.

If you still struggle to believe in abundance, you might face challenges in achieving your aspirations. Let's review the characteristics of individuals who lack belief in abundance:

1. Low self-esteem

2. Doubt in their own abilities

3. Tendency towards self-destructive thoughts rather than affirming self-beliefs

4. Unstable beliefs

5. Fragile self-confidence

6. A mean-spirited approach towards life

7. Cognitive distortions

8. Resistance to learning and change

9. Absence of ethical living

Take a moment to reflect on the above points to identify your own beliefs and see if they align with the abundance mindset. If you recognise traits that oppose abundance in your thinking, it's time to reconsider your beliefs. For instance, if you lack belief in your abilities, you limit yourself. But by recognising your inherent talents and acquired skills, you'll realise the extraordinary potential you possess. At that point, your approach to asking will change significantly. Embrace your strengths, follow your capabilities, and maintain unwavering faith in abundance. The world is ready to bestow its most beautiful and rewarding offerings. With the right mindset and belief in abundance, your path to success and fulfilment will be paved with opportunities.

Chapter 3
Methods

A person with high self-confidence but lacking swimming skills will drown if they jump into the sea.

Third chapter

Methods

Although we discussed techniques in previous chapters, I will introduce some new techniques in this section to help you achieve your final goal.

In the earlier chapters, we emphasised the importance of redefining words. We explained that failures, mental illnesses, and undesirable behaviours often result from misinterpreting words. To overcome these issues, we need to analyse words and their meanings. Additionally, we explored our existential powers to gain insight into our abilities and potential for personal growth and development. The techniques introduced in the last chapter focused on abundance, teaching us to change our perspective and recognise the possibilities within ourselves and the world. This change in mindset is crucial for laying the foundation for our future endeavours.

Another critical topic in this book is the concept of "wanting". Redefining words, understanding our existential powers, and embracing abundance are essential, but we will not achieve our goals without a strong desire. There is a strong relationship between analysing words and the concepts of power and abundance, and they continuously reinforce each other. Ultimately, desire becomes the driving force that helps us achieve our goals.

This chapter will delve deeper into the necessary steps to achieve our goals. While redefining words, recognising existential strengths, building self-confidence, and embracing abundance are essential prerequisites, they require effort. Understanding the verb "want" better and moving towards our goal with self-confidence and practical methods are equally crucial. We have developed confidence and a strong desire in previous sections, and now we are ready to explore the realm of methodology.

Understanding the power of desire and the art of manifestation is vital. By absorbing the lessons of the previous chapters and applying practical methods, you are set up for success. To achieve better results, it's important to continue practising the exercises of the previous chapters and implementing the techniques presented in this chapter.

Rereading technique

The main idea of this book is that words play a significant role in shaping people's lives. Throughout the book, it is demonstrated how a single word can have different meanings for different individuals. Words can create feelings, knowledge, motivation, meaning, and behaviour, and it is impossible for a single word to have the same effect on everyone. For instance, the word "rain" evokes different feelings in different people, leading to varying motivations and behaviours in response to rain. Despite this individual variation, people often try to ascribe an ordinary meaning to words, oversimplifying their complexities. However, a word's psychological and emotional impact varies significantly from person to person.

Someone who leaves home on a rainy day due to a personal conflict has a different emotional response to rain than someone who grew up in a desert or experienced a flood. Therefore, although the word "rain" may have the same physical reference, it holds different psychological, emotional, and cognitive meanings for different individuals. This challenge becomes even more pronounced when dealing with words that do not have a physical form, such as "God," "success," "good," "bad," and numerous other similar words, each carrying various cognitive, psychological, and emotional connotations. People shape their lives based on these interpretations, resulting in diverse definitions for these abstract concepts. Consequently, each person's understanding and experience of these words are unique, influencing their behaviours, emotions, and psychological responses. It is essential to recognise that the meaning of a word is not inherent but is shaped by numerous factors. Furthermore, the diverse definitions of abstract concepts like "success" are influenced by many factors, such as religious beliefs, family upbringing, and educational and societal environments. As a result, each person's interpretation of success varies, leading to different perceptions of success and failure.

SPEAR Techniques

The first technique we will talk about is the "SPEAR" technique. We should be able to learn how to use a spear, aim it at our target, and throw it with precision. This technique is about examining the "word" and knowing exactly what that word is. As we said earlier, people think they precisely understand words. Still, after careful examination, they realise that their words are contaminated by family, environmental, educational, and cognitive beliefs. This contamination causes that word to play a negative role in their lives. So, the first technique to achieve significant achievements or success is to define your goal and carefully examine the word that fits it. For this purpose, five essential steps must be taken.

S: First, you should consider a specific goal and draw a specific word out of that goal. S means "special word," for example, my goal is to become a doctor. This is my specific goal. Of course, it can be made more specific, such as a neurologist, cardiologist, or other specialities. Each of them should be checked using the technique specified. The first thing to do is to examine the specific word. The special word here is "doctor." Maybe you all believe this word does not need to be examined, and everyone knows what a doctor is, but you will see further that the matter is not as easy as we think. Is the definition of a doctor by an obsessive person the same as an average person? Doesn't this definition change by a person who is sensitive to blood or a person who is afraid of seeing a wound? If a person has an artistic spirit but cannot discover it, can he become a doctor? Many examples show that some people have stopped working and started other jobs after continuing their education and obtaining a medical degree.

I had a client who was complaining about his child's disvalue. When I asked him why his child lacked value, he said that he is a dentist, but after receiving a dental degree, he opened a coffee shop and is not willing to work as a dentist. Now, the matter is becoming clear. Similar issues with my client show that not everyone has the same definition of a dentist.

For example, how can a person who vomits and panics when he sees people's mouths become a dentist? The continuation of the meeting with the client showed that family pressure had caused their child to study dentistry to please his parents. Still, after graduation, he showed his parents that he had fulfilled his commitment but could not work in this field. In fact, this person had wasted more than five years of his life. If this person had known the technique of "psychotherapist's words" before starting his studies, he would not have wasted his life.

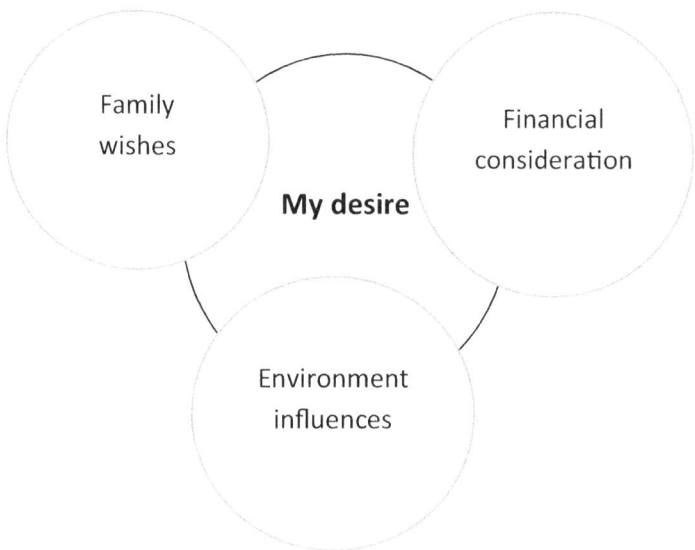

Carefully, in the picture above, we can see how this person's definition of the word "dentist" was contaminated by external factors such as family wishes, financial considerations, and environmental influences. In order to make the right decision, this person must clean these contaminations. The method is to attach his definition to the word without external considerations. For example, he should first check his family's bias towards becoming a dentist and ask himself such questions. Will my parents do dentistry, or will I? If I am not interested in this field, will family pressures create interest or not? If I am uncomfortable with this subject during teaching, will I be hurt by my parents?

Only the answer to these questions can remove the pollution caused by family pressure, and the person will conclude that family pressure will not bring anything except a waste of time, energy, and mental damage.

Now, in order to be able to eliminate the pollution resulting from financial considerations, he must ask himself other regular questions. For example, these questions can be asked: Is the only field of dentistry profitable? Are all dentists rich? Are other jobs not profitable? Is the income from dentistry worth enough to hurt my psyche? By answering the above questions, one can come to the conclusion that other jobs can be as profitable as dentistry. My client said that his son's income from the coffee shop is very high, and he wants to establish other branches, but the family does not support his job.

As you can see, with the related questions, we removed the family contamination and the contamination resulting from financial considerations. In the same way, you can clean other contaminations as well. After that, we will have a precise cognitive definition of the word "dentist." For example, my client's definition will be that dentistry is a good academic field that can earn a good income, but he has no desire to work as a dentist. Under this definition, he also writes his reasons. As I said earlier, the reasons for each person are different, and when the reasons are written, the person knows that this field is not for him.

The above case was negative, but we should continue using the same method for positive cases. For example, after removing the external factors that led him to become a dentist, a person expresses his definition of this word and concludes that this field is his favourite. This person also writes his reasons, and after examining his reasons, he concludes that dentistry is the best job for him.

P: The second thing we need to do with a word is to know what parallel definitions have been given about that word. For example, we examine the word "success." Each person's definition of success is different. However, people's desire for material things has caused most people to consider success as earning money. However, as I showed in the article above, these definitions are due to the pollution that the environment, family, and society impose on us. To better understand the word, it is better to see the word from different angles and understand how a word can have parallel definitions.

Instead of using case studies, I usually peruse words by reading books. But you can also use case studies. For example, if your target word is "success," before you follow the standard definition, it is better to identify the people whom you think are successful. You will get valuable insights if you can briefly talk with them and see if they consider themselves successful. The results of these conversations might be similar to the following:

- I am successful in the financial field, but I have many problems in the family field.
- Getting a good academic rank did not give me a better life. However, I thought I would achieve great success by getting a good rank and studying at a good university.
- I am lucky; my family supports me and loves me a lot, but I don't have a good income from work.
- I have a good business but don't consider myself successful because I have big goals.
- I am a successful person because I do what I love.

You can add hundreds more to the above. However, since my method is aimed at studying, I try to consider success from a philosophical point of view. For example, what is the definition of success by philosophers like Socrates and Aristotle or the new philosophers? What is the view of religions on success? What do successful people, such as Gandhi and Elon Musk, look at success? What did the Stoics think about success?

After listing all the above items, I will have a precise definition of success. The result of this research will be not to confuse achievement with success. For example, a person who has achieved great wealth but has not been able to have a successful family has confused achievement with success. It can be said that he had exemplary achievements, but it cannot be said that he was successful. By examining the world, we will be able to have a good balance in our lives and walk our paths with more confidence.

E: Consider which word is enchanting or enthusiastic and is in harmony with your mood. Humans are unique, and each person's interests are different from another. After checking the parallel definitions, you should see which can be fascinating and make you enthusiastic to reach that definition. For example, if I come across different definitions of "success," some of which consider success to be the acquisition of wealth, this definition is not fascinating to me. But if I find definitions that define success as being valuable and effective, this definition excites me, and I try to see if what I am doing will lead me to be effective or not. A person who sees success only as acquiring wealth will not be pleased with my orientation. Therefore, this person should see which definition fascinates them. For example, if a person considers success to be the acquisition of wealth, they will not need to love their job because their ultimate goal is wealth, and anything and every action that can bring them wealth will be pleasing to them. So, in the first step, be sensitive to the enthusiastic and enchanting words.

A: Acceptability is another thing to consider. After putting together new definitions from the latest knowledge we acquire, we must see which definition is compatible with our spirit. Which definition can lead us to more joy and reduce our sorrow? Which definition does not conflict with my core beliefs? Of course, our core beliefs are sometimes problematic, and we must reconsider them. However, suppose after reconsidering and recognising our moods, we feel that a definition is incompatible with our spirit and moods. In that case, we should avoid that definition and adopt one that can create happiness and lead us to our desired success, supported by intellectual backing.

R: The flexibility and reasonableness of the definitions should be examined at the end. I have said before that when examining words, we must set aside the beliefs imposed by culture, family, and environment, but this is very difficult, and these beliefs sneak into our minds. Therefore, ultimately, we must review the desired definition and see if it was chosen based on logic and conscious reasoning or if external beliefs still contaminate it. For example, if someone has Islamic inclinations and takes the definition of success from fanatical and strict Islamic clerics, they may be wrong. For instance, a person who becomes interested in ISIS may think that killing those he believes to be infidels means success, believing he will enter heaven by doing this. But is this belief true or contaminated by external beliefs imposed on his mind? Similarly, someone who examines the life of a smuggler and thinks that getting rich through smuggling made him happy can have a wrong definition of success. So, in the last step, we must see if our definitions are accessible from the insidious beliefs placed in our minds or adopted without their influence.

SMART Techniques

After the "SPEAR" technique, it is time for the SMART technique. This technique has been mentioned many times in different books and theories before this book, but in my opinion, it works better when we have learned the "SPEAR" technique. The SMART technique cannot be used effectively without redefining the words that lead to a change in knowledge.

For example, the mere desire to acquire wealth lacks a universal formula for success. As a result, many people are frustrated by their inability to realise their dreams because they do not have a correct definition of their desired subject. They must first understand the word for themselves and then reach the second stage, the SMART stage.

Reviewing SMART goals at this stage holds significant importance. SMART goals, an acronym for Specific, Measurable, Achievable, Realistic, and Timely, provide a practical framework for setting effective goals. Among these elements, specificity is particularly vital. I prioritise understanding their specific goals when working with clients who have experienced consistent failures. Many clients have a general idea but lack a clear target. For instance, they might express a desire to become a merchant, but when asked about the specific type of merchant they aspire to be, they struggle to provide a concrete answer. This lack of specificity is akin to an eagle being hungry and in need of food yet unsure about which prey to pursue or where to find it. Consequently, the eagle aimlessly soars through the sky, spotting various animals in the field but unable to seize them due to indecision. Thus, the first step in this method is to establish a clear and specific goal.

This can be achieved through the following points:

1. Identify successful people who have excelled in your chosen field.
2. Study their success methods and strategies by examining their biographies.

3. Determine the key factors that contributed to their achievements.

4. Learn how to obtain and visualise these success factors.

5. Develop an action plan based on the acquired knowledge and understanding of success factors.

Additionally, it is crucial to have a thorough understanding of the measurability of your goal. Deluding oneself about capabilities will not lead to progress. For example, to become a merchant, you should create a well-defined timetable and allocate dedicated time each day, week, month, and year to your pursuit. Furthermore, the achievability of your goal should be carefully considered. Is it realistically attainable? Just as an eagle contemplating the prospect of preying on an elephant must assess its ability to execute such a feat and the subsequent challenge of carrying the massive prey to its nest, you, too, must evaluate the feasibility of your objective. It is essential to document the entire timetable of your journey.

In the fourth step, your goal should be realistic. Similar to an eagle preparing for a strenuous struggle if it aims to prey on an elephant, if your aspiration as a merchant involves trading expensive goods that you cannot afford to purchase, it would be an impractical idea. Realism should serve as a guiding principle throughout your goal-setting process. Lastly, all these aspects should be incorporated into a structured timetable and time framework. Following this method will set you on a path to success. However, it is essential to note that while all five elements are necessary, they alone are insufficient. I will provide a more detailed explanation of additional techniques in subsequent discussions.

Stay calm and composed. The challenges mentioned above can be efficiently addressed without consuming excessive time. The key lies in establishing a sense of regulation and discipline. Below, you will find a comprehensive set of techniques that will equip you to overcome these obstacles effectively. Take the time to peruse and absorb the information provided thoroughly.

Meticulously documenting and extensively researching

To effectively pursue practical matters, conducting thorough investigations and developing a comprehensive understanding of your goals and the necessary methods is imperative. Taking action is critical, but it is essential to acknowledge that reaching the action stage involves several preparatory steps. It is required to accurately document the answers to the abovementioned questions and articulate one's talents and abilities with precision. Diligent research should be conducted to minimise errors. While some motivational psychologists propagate the belief that individuals can accomplish anything, it is crucial to recognise our limitations to avoid setbacks. In line with **Jean-Paul Sartre's** assertion that "Man is condemned to freedom," every human being possesses this freedom, even individuals with physical disabilities. For instance, while a disabled person may face challenges competing in a sprint race without assistive devices, they should not lose motivation or the desire to participate. Instead, they must recognise their capabilities and strive to find alternative ways to engage in the competition. Participating in the Paralympic Games, where all athletes have similar disabilities, or exploring the invention of a device that leverages their thigh muscles to facilitate running are potential avenues to consider.

To begin, it is crucial to clearly articulate your goals and aspirations, drawing upon your personal determination. A relevant example is Donald Trump, who ventured into constructing a golf course despite lacking prior experience in the field. Through meticulous examination of his desires, he recognised that this pursuit aligned with his primary occupation of building apartments. Furthermore, he committed himself to extensive research in order to overcome challenges.

In his book, "Trump Never Give Up!", Trump recounts his encounter with opposition from the Scottish government when proposing the construction of a golf course. Undeterred, he and his team dedicated countless hours to studying the project, delving into the reasons behind the government's reluctance. They developed enticing and advantageous plans despite the initially unfavourable prospects. Eventually, their comprehensive proposal effectively demonstrated its merits to the municipality, leading to a remarkable shift from opposition to enthusiastic agreement. This anecdote underscores the significance of maintaining a clear vision throughout our endeavours. In the face of any issues within our plans, it is essential to address them through consultation and strategic adjustment.

After meticulously documenting and extensively researching your goals, the time for action has arrived. Let us consider the example of aspiring to become a successful chef. Merely working in an ordinary restaurant would not suffice. To position yourself within society as a chef, you must delve deeper into the lives of accomplished chefs and understand their methodologies for success. By honing your culinary skills and practical abilities, you can be well-prepared to avoid potential embarrassment or setbacks. However, with an unwavering belief in your ability to excel as a top-tier chef, you can showcase your talents on various platforms. Embracing creativity is critical – perhaps you can incorporate musical elements by serenading patrons while serving food. The possibilities for innovation are endless. Gradually, word will spread about your unique approach, and it won't be long before you gain recognition as a renowned chef.

By clearly defining your objectives and aligning them with your ambitions, you embark on the path to success.

The practical steps to achieve success one by one:

Get training

The Significance of Training and Continuous Learning for Professional Advancement

The significance of training and continuous learning cannot be overstated when achieving success in any professional endeavour. Even seemingly straightforward tasks require a certain level of training and proficiency to excel. This principle holds across a wide range of professions, including the role of wait staff in the restaurant industry. To become a successful waiter, one must first acquire the necessary skills in effectively utilising detergents and cleaners. Often, individuals who express dissatisfaction with their lack of success lack the essential expertise required for their respective fields. However, there are also cases where individuals possess expertise but struggle to leverage it effectively. In either scenario, prioritising learning and continuous improvement becomes paramount in attaining one's goals.

The Importance of Comprehensive Learning:

To illustrate this point further, let us consider the aspirations of a cook. Aspiring cooks must acquire culinary skills and master various cooking techniques to thrive in their profession. For instance, someone living in a multicultural country like England, with diverse food preferences, must specialise in a particular cuisine while maintaining proficiency in other culinary domains. Learning encompasses a vast scope, and no one can claim to have mastered every aspect of a specific field. Moreover, as one acquires more knowledge and skills, they become more adept at attracting and engaging others.

Acquiring knowledge of the art of food decoration and cooking skills are crucial. In the culinary industry, food presentation holds significant weight in attracting customers, particularly those with discerning tastes. Thus, investing substantial time in learning how to decorate food skilfully becomes paramount. Mastery in this area enables chefs to showcase their creativity and captivate diners' attention. Pursuing education in this domain knows no bounds, as increased creativity generates heightened interest and intrigue.

The Multifaceted Nature of Expertise:

Becoming a renowned chef and achieving financial success requires extensive training and a dedicated commitment to learning. Ambitious individuals must possess the willingness to endure challenges and embrace ongoing development. What may initially appear as a simple task, such as cooking, is a complex endeavour requiring a diverse skill set. Fortunately, most of these abilities can be acquired through dedicated learning efforts. While creativity may seem inherently innate, studying the techniques employed by creative individuals can inspire unique designs. Personal creativity flourishes by exposing oneself to various innovative methods, leading to the development of an individualised approach.

Through perseverance and continuous learning, aspiring professionals can emerge as chefs whose reputation resonates with others, thereby unlocking the doors to success and becoming proficient and successful demands an unwavering commitment to training encompassing various aspects of the chosen field. Each skill acquired, and every lesson learned contributes to an individual's growth and enhances their ability to attract others. Therefore, aspiring professionals should embrace the value of training and recognise the transformative power of continuous learning on their path to prosperity.

1- Be disciplined

The importance of discipline should never be underestimated, as it plays a critical role in achieving success. Throughout history, only a select few individuals have achieved remarkable accomplishments without discipline. This fact becomes evident when we analyse the underlying reasons.

Discipline encompasses adhering to a specific path and firmly believing in it. Those who disregard the significance of discipline tend to rely on external motivation and easily succumb to their emotions. Their actions are primarily driven by fleeting excitement, which they often derive from external sources. As a result, their behaviour fluctuates, characterised by sporadic bursts of enthusiasm followed by periods of inaction. As mentioned earlier, progress towards a goal inevitably involves encountering obstacles and problems.

In contrast, individuals who embrace discipline perceive challenges as integral components of the journey towards success. They exhibit a sense of contentment when dealing with problems, similar to their state of comfort. Such individuals view obstacles as opportunities for growth and learning. Consequently, their minds remain consistently focused on their goals, resulting in a sense of order and structure.

Conversely, individuals lacking discipline are prone to laziness and solely seek comfort. When faced with a problem, they become pessimistic and display a negative attitude. As Donald Trump aptly stated, "Negativeness is easy for lazy people." However, discipline is far from easy. It requires actively combating laziness and maintaining a strong sense of commitment.

A person lacking discipline adheres to no specific routine. They wake up and work at their convenience, engaging in social activities whenever they please. Due to the absence of discipline in their behaviour, they fail to achieve consistent results. On the other hand, individuals who adhere to a regular and disciplined lifestyle obligate themselves to act in alignment with their goals regardless of the circumstances. They do not complain about fatigue, nor do they fear challenges. Even in the most adverse conditions, they maintain a consistent work schedule, dedicating themselves to their objectives.

People who practice discipline are known for their reliability. They convey a message to those around them that they are trustworthy and committed to fulfilling their obligations and agreements. External factors hold no power over their determination, preventing them from succumbing to laziness or displaying improper conduct. Therefore, discipline entails assigning value to the goal and having an unwavering belief in its achievement.

To illustrate the significance of the order in reaching goals, we can examine the behaviour of small creatures such as ants. Despite their diminutive size, ants exemplify the effectiveness of discipline and perseverance. In the harshest winters, these diligent insects tirelessly transport seeds, often their own weight, to their nests, ensuring their survival. These industrious creatures would inevitably perish without discipline due to a lack of food. Nature has taught them that discipline, perseverance, and persistence are indispensable elements of success.

2- Embracing Perseverance:

It is crucial to recognise that achieving success is a process that unfolds over time rather than an instantaneous event. While it is true that some individuals may experience sudden recognition for various reasons, it is not imprudent to rely solely on chance to determine one's fate. Persistence is a vital and indispensable element in the pursuit of success.

For instance, if you have established a personal presence on a platform, expecting a significant audience to gather within days, weeks, or even months is unrealistic. Building visibility and influence may require years of dedicated effort. Individuals who hold onto immediate rewards often find themselves quickly disheartened. They expect substantial returns from minimal investments and abandon their endeavours when immediate results fail to materialise.

It is worth noting that Donald Trump once acknowledged that some of his plans took as long as three decades to come to fruition. While I am not advocating for such an extended waiting period, the message remains clear. If you genuinely believe in your chosen path, backed by thorough research and analysis indicating that success is attainable, it is essential not to surrender. Persevere on your chosen path until the obstacles to success lose their potency and succumb to your unwavering determination.

Remember that the strength behind closed doors pales compared to the power you possess within yourself. With relentless persistence, victory is undoubtedly within your reach.

3- Close your ears, open your eyes
You will come out of the well

Commencing this part, let us begin with a captivating anecdote as a valuable illustration. According to legend, five mice were trapped in a sizable water-filled hole. A crowd gathered around the pit, eagerly observing the mice's plight and contemplating their escape. Despite the immense challenge before them, the determined rodents exhibited unwavering perseverance. However, the crowd sought to undermine their resolve, vocally asserting that the mice were destined to perish, unable to overcome their predicament. Eventually, all but one of the mice succumbed to the mounting pressure and met their demise. The onlookers, quick to highlight the perceived futility of the mice's efforts, were astounded when the lone survivor, against all odds, emerged from the pit. Curiosity piqued, the spectators approached the triumphant mouse, eager to unravel the secret behind its success. To their surprise, the mouse paid no attention to their inquiries—it was deaf.

This fable imparts a valuable principle: one should not heed the opinions and discouragement of others. More often than not, people's endeavours revolve around maintaining their superiority and limiting the achievements of others to match their level of optimism. Only a select few genuinely strive to foster the success of others. Thus, it is crucial to recognise that the first advocate for your goals should be yourself. While seeking advice and assistance from others can be beneficial, excessive dependency on them will divert you from your desired goal. Relying too heavily on others engenders weakness and undermines your sense of self-worth while fostering independence, which enables self-assurance and the ability to leverage others' guidance to uncover more significant opportunities. By relying on your abilities, you retain the capacity to seek assistance when necessary. However, if others perceive you as dependent, not only will they withhold their aid, but they will also perpetuate your reliance on them.

Consequently, it is essential to remember that most individuals struggle to tolerate the triumphs of others. Although it may seem somewhat tangential to delve into this topic within the confines of a psychology book, psychological experiments have unfortunately demonstrated that people tend to harbour an aversion to witnessing others surpass them. Since the advent of civilisation and the transition from a nomadic existence to a more interconnected society, the propensity for comparative self-assessment has given rise to envy among individuals.

While our discussion does not explicitly revolve around jealousy, it is pertinent to elucidate that jealousy is an inherent human trait. Remarkably, studies have shown that infants possess the potential for jealousy. Multiple investigations [1] have revealed that infants as young as six months exhibit behaviours indicative of jealousy. For instance, when their mothers interact with another infant or engage in play with a doll, these infants manifest anger and direct it towards their mothers.

Hence, it is unwise to anticipate the unwavering support and applause of others as a prerequisite for success. Only those who are genuinely interested in your endeavours will encourage you. Moreover, during this journey, your family can be a source of support and motivation, although not everyone is fortunate enough to possess such unwavering familial backing.

---

[1] **Hart S, Carrington HA (2002) Jealousy in six-month-old infants. Infancy 3: 395–402.**

4- Having a sponsor is necessary but not essential

This discourse addresses the issue of individuals seeking encouragement and assistance from others to achieve success, as well as the potential feelings of discouragement and depression that may arise from rejected requests. Many individuals have approached me, expressing that the absence of a sponsor is the primary reason for their lack of success. While having a sponsor is a crucial and fundamental opportunity, it is worth exploring the possibility of attaining abundance without one.

Let us envision a scenario where you possess a treasure map that, once discovered, has the potential to transform your life. However, unearthing this treasure requires advanced equipment, which can be likened to the sponsor role. If we do not have a sponsor, does it imply that the treasure does not exist? Certainly not. The only aspect that changes is our approach to reaching the treasure. Even in the face of criticism or discouragement from friends and family, their opinions do not determine abundance availability. This is the moment to tune out their voices and open our eyes. While they express their opinions, we must remain determined to achieve our goals. Exploring alternative paths that can lead us to our objectives is crucial.

Professor **Steven Hayes**, the founder of Acceptance and Commitment Therapy (ACT), proposes that when we feel lonely, hurt by others, or burdened by constant blame, we should reflect on the values that govern our lives. These values can serve as guiding principles that prevent us from falling into despair. For instance, I value contributing something to this world that fosters peace. My interest in wealth is rooted in this life value, as I aspire to uplift those in poverty. Recognising the importance of this value, even in the absence of support from others, I must forge my own path. Steven Hayes offers a practical solution, drawing from ancient Stoic wisdom. He advises us to cultivate self-awareness through the practice of mindfulness.

Mindfulness entails consciously directing our attention, with openness, interest, and acceptance, towards our present experiences. Therefore, if we find ourselves alone in the challenging journey toward success, with others attempting to undermine our efforts, the first step is to deepen our understanding of ourselves through mindfulness. We can overcome adversity by acknowledging the challenges along the path, diligently planning, and persistently striving.

Hence, it is possible to achieve success without relying on others. The key lies in discovering our own unique path. Below, I will outline a few essential factors that should be considered:

1. Set clear goals: Clearly define your objectives precisely and clearly.
2. Develop a strategic plan: Create a roadmap outlining the steps and actions required to achieve your goals.
3. Cultivate resilience: Embrace setbacks as learning opportunities and persist in facing obstacles.
4. Seek knowledge and self-improvement: Continuously acquire new skills, expand your knowledge base, and invest in personal growth.
5. Build a support network: While self-reliance is essential, surrounding yourself with like-minded

individuals who share your aspirations can provide encouragement and inspiration.

6. Stay focused and maintain mindfulness: Direct your attention and energy towards your goals while accepting the challenges and difficulties that may arise.

7. Adapt and adjust: Be flexible and willing to modify strategies if necessary while remaining true to your core values and purpose.

Remember, success is within your reach, even in a challenging journey. By practising mindfulness, accepting the inherent difficulties, and diligently planning and striving, you can pave your own way to success.

5- Focus like a lion

Mindfulness, a concept often observed instinctively in animals such as lions during their hunts, offers valuable lessons for human beings. By cultivating an understanding and appreciation of the present moment, we can significantly enhance our ability to concentrate and effectively pursue our goals. This article explores the virtues of mindfulness, including the practice of living in the present and developing concentration, and how they can aid in overcoming depression, anxiety, and distractions.

Living in the Present:

Many individuals who encounter repeated setbacks in life tend to dwell either on past failures, leading to depression, or on future uncertainties, causing anxiety. However, mindfulness encourages us to direct our attention to the present moment. Recognising that the past is behind us and the future is yet to unfold, we can train ourselves to stay grounded in the here and now. This practice enables us to alleviate depression and anxiety, fostering a more fulfilling and contented life.

Developing Concentration:

Living in the present empowers us to clear our minds of ineffective and unnecessary thoughts. Those who embrace mindfulness no longer fixate on past mistakes or obsess over future concerns. Instead, they filter out irrelevant information, allowing their minds to focus on essential matters. For example, an aspiring writer can channel their attention toward refining their writing technique, disregarding extraneous distractions.

Distinguishing Vital Information:

A fundamental aspect of mindfulness involves discerning crucial information from the overwhelming sea of data we encounter daily. Separating and prioritising various inputs avoids wasting time and energy on irrelevant details. This enables us to invest our resources in what truly matters, propelling us closer to our objectives. Consequently, we cultivate a focused mind that can concentrate on a single subject rather than succumbing to whims and confusion, ultimately accelerating our progress towards our goals.

Practising mindfulness empowers us to recognise the significance of the present moment and concentrate on what truly matters. By consciously living in the now, we can overcome the burdens of depression and anxiety, leading to a more fulfilling life. Furthermore, mindfulness lets us clear our minds of distractions, allowing us to focus on our primary objectives. Through this intentional separation of vital information, we allocate our resources wisely, moving towards our goals with clarity and efficiency. Embracing mindfulness as a tool for personal growth and success is a powerful step toward achieving our aspirations.

6- Absorb small powers

In the journey towards our goals, we must acknowledge that each of us possesses unique strengths and abilities. However, we must not overlook even the smallest of these powers, as they can significantly influence our path to success. Let us avoid being overly romantic and focus on identifying and embracing our inherent abilities, no matter how tiny they may seem.

For instance, consider the power of determination. When you set your sights on a goal, recognise that your determination is a force that can drive you forward. In your journey, take a moment to acknowledge this power by writing down, "Determination is my first power" on your table. By doing so, you begin to rely on and appreciate this aspect of yourself.

But don't stop there—continue exploring and discovering more of your strengths. Each small power you recognise and absorb contributes to your overall progress. It could be your ability to stay resilient in the face of challenges or your creative problem-solving skills. Embrace these powers, document them, and let them fuel your journey towards accomplishing your goals. Understanding and leveraging these abilities can create a formidable foundation for your success.

Remember, success is not solely achieved through grand gestures or sweeping changes. Often, the accumulation and appreciation of the little powers within ourselves propel us forward. So, let us embark on this empowering journey of self-discovery and growth, one small power at a time.

Our analysis shows that we often underestimate the substantial capabilities at our disposal, leading to a pervasive sense of powerlessness. This failure can be primarily attributed to a misperception of our own potential. To rectify this, let us establish power as the ability to accomplish tasks. Consider the following actions: running, writing, driving, and speaking. Each action necessitates a specific skill set, which we call power. For instance, the physical strength of my muscles enables me to run, while my proficiency in reading and writing empowers me to engage in these activities. Consequently, power plays an integral role in the conjugation of verbs, as without it, no task can be successfully achieved.

Returning to our core subject of goal pursuit, we must acknowledge that attaining any objective requires strength. During my interactions with numerous individuals, I have encountered those who approach me with grievances about their perceived limitations. In response, I consistently advise them to articulate their aspirations in writing. Frequently, their goals lack ambition, with some aspiring to become teachers, open a shop, or pursue a medical career. Despite the brevity of my consultations with these individuals, a remarkable transformation has occurred in their lives. How? By initiating a dialogue with an individual aspiring to become a teacher, I prompted him to reflect upon his inherent strengths. Did he possess the necessary power to fulfil his aspirations? If so, which institution validated this power? Although he admitted to lacking the requisite qualifications, he exhibited great motivation and interest. Together, we explored avenues through which he could acquire the power of teaching. He identified institutions offering free teacher training, and in subsequent meetings, he revealed his enrolment in these courses. Eventually, after two years, he realised his dream of becoming a full-time teacher.

Merely harbouring wishes or envisioning a desired outcome will prove insufficient in pursuing your goals. It is imperative to acquire the requisite strength to transform them into reality. Begin by defining your objectives and discerning the specific powers necessary for their achievement. Diligently investigate how these powers can be acquired and actively take steps towards them. By doing so, you will steadily progress towards your goals, ultimately culminating in their successful attainment.

7- Do stupid things, and don't be afraid of the opposition

When **Henry Ford** introduced his visionary concept of the motor vehicle to the world, he was met with widespread scepticism and ridicule. However, Ford possessed a deep understanding that transcended the doubts of his critics. He firmly believed in the limitless potential of abundance and recognised the power of transforming ideas into reality. Unfazed by the mockery he faced, Ford tenaciously pursued his chosen path, undeterred by the numerous instances of ridicule he encountered.

Similarly, Donald Trump has encountered significant ridicule throughout his life, with many questioning his sanity and unorthodox approach. As a businessman, he ventured into obscure and seemingly unprofitable projects, drawing criticism from those who doubted his judgment. Even upon assuming the presidency, Trump faced widespread opposition to his leadership. Nevertheless, his determination remained unwavering. In 1976, he made a surprising move to acquire the Grand Hyatt Hotel on the grounds of the bankrupt Penn Central Railroad Commodore Hotel, a decision that earned him scorn from sceptics. Disregarding the chorus of naysayers, Trump meticulously assessed the situation, drawing upon his own understanding and seeking counsel from his father's wisdom. Ultimately, he invested without regret, shutting out the desperate voices that opposed him and remaining open to the possibilities.

During his presidential time, he encountered opponents. Among his opponents were notable figures who openly criticised him. Renowned scientist **Stephen Hawking** referred to Trump as a demagogue who seemed to appeal to the lowest common denominator. Actor **Robert De Niro** expressed disbelief that someone like Trump could hold such a position, describing his statements as outrageous, ridiculous, and indicative of an unhinged individual. In an interview with London's Channel 5 News, **Johnny Depp** voiced his concerns about a Trump presidency, suggesting that it would signal the end of an era for the United States. **George Clooney**, in an interview with The Guardian, denounced Trump as an opportunist and labelled him a xenophobic fascist, contending that extreme ideas often surface during election seasons but rarely come to fruition.

While an entire book could be devoted to chronicling Trump's adversaries, the focus here is not to scrutinise his life but to examine his methods of success. Upon reading Trump's autobiography, one cannot help but notice that he encountered more dissenting voices than supportive ones throughout his life. However, these opponents held no sway in impeding the progress of his plans. The lesson to be gleaned from this is clear: if you face blame or ridicule, it is crucial to brush it off and forge ahead. With unwavering conviction, implement your vision. Believe in your plan, fearlessly execute it, and be assured that victory will eventually be yours. Tune out disparaging voices and remain attuned to the possibilities that surround you. Even if success eludes you initially, persist and learn from each attempt, for it is through perseverance that triumph is ultimately achieved.

8- Don't be hasty

Albert Einstein famously stated, "The successes that patient individuals achieve are the ones that hasty individuals abandon." Attaining success requires developing inner strength, which can only be achieved through continuous improvement and diligent effort. This transformative process demands considerable time and dedication. For instance, envisioning and owning a restaurant necessitates extensive research, such as visiting multiple establishments and seeking opinions, which typically spans several months. However, establishing and managing a restaurant requires years of unwavering commitment and perseverance.

To embark on this journey, one must first augment their knowledge of restaurant management and acquire adequate culinary training. Subsequently, securing the necessary funds becomes paramount in establishing the restaurant. The subsequent step entails meticulously studying different locations and selecting the most suitable one while comprehending the local market demands. Each of these stages demands a significant investment of time. Furthermore, it is crucial to recognise that setbacks and failures may still arise even after the restaurant has been designed and established. In such instances, it is imperative to exercise patience, analyse mistakes, and make the necessary adjustments. The ability to repeatedly start afresh with unwavering resilience is of utmost importance.

If you have not achieved success thus far, it is plausible that impatience may have hindered your progress. Did you surrender after encountering the initial setback? Did initial negative feedback dishearten you? It is crucial to reflect upon your past actions. Analyse the initiatives you undertook and the reasons behind abandoning them. Was it premature to declare failure? Could you have persisted further in resolving the challenges? Did you seek guidance from others to overcome obstacles? If your answer to these questions is affirmative, then impatience may have played a role. However, there is no cause for concern. As mentioned earlier, it is essential not to surrender, and if you stumble, you must be prepared to start anew. The key to success lies in faith in your abilities and chosen goal. If you possess a belief in your own capabilities and have selected a goal driven by passion and genuine interest, then it is imperative to initiate the journey once again. Avoid the temptation to rush this time.

Fear is an innate emotion experienced by all individuals. However, successful individuals do not allow fear to control their actions. They perceive fear as a cautionary signal. Primary fear alerts us to potential dangers or mistakes, while secondary fear is a byproduct of being afraid. Understanding primary fear enables us to solve problems, whereas secondary fear paralyses us. Hence, it is crucial not to fear your own fear. Instead, strive to identify its signs and underlying causes. For instance, if you have invested in a business and fear the prospect of bankruptcy, can you be afraid to prevent such an outcome? If fear serves as a warning to keep you vigilant, should you not appreciate its presence? You should abstain from fearing fear and value the vigilance it instils. This concept is observable in the animal kingdom as well. When a prey animal senses danger, it flees to escape the predator. However, if the prey succumbs to its own fear and misinterprets it as surrender, it becomes paralysed, losing the ability to escape. Similarly, soldiers on the battlefield experience fear. Some soldiers respond by acknowledging the warning and preserving their safety, while others succumb to fear and secondary excitement, resulting in paralysis. Survivors among the latter group often recount complete immobilisation, unable to move their legs.

Occasionally, fear can be a catalyst for success. However, it is vital to embrace your fears and seek solutions to overcome the challenges they present. If you validate your fears, failure becomes inevitable. Therefore, navigate through the various stages of success, acknowledging that numerous obstacles will arise. Without succumbing to fear, strive to find solutions and persist.

9- Just start

Congratulations, you've come to the end of this book armed with newfound knowledge and techniques to propel you forward. However, there's one crucial lesson that you must never forget: "just start." As you've absorbed the wisdom contained within these pages, remember that knowledge, techniques, and ambition alone are not enough. It's time to put the book away and embark on your journey.

Throughout your voyage, you may encounter challenges that test your resolve, and there might be moments when you feel like giving up. In those times of doubt, don't hesitate to revisit this book. Allow its words to reignite the fire within you and remind you of your purpose.

Sometimes, your inner voice may encourage you to rest, and that's okay. Listen to yourself, and take the time you need. But when the moment is right, muster the strength to continue your journey. Like a hungry eagle, waiting for others to bring you meat won't suffice. Instead, soar high in the sky, observe your surroundings, and go after your goals with determination.

As the author of this book, I will be immensely proud if you take that first step and start your journey. So, embrace the spirit of an ambitious eagle, and let your aspirations guide you towards new heights. The world is waiting for you to spread your wings and soar. Go forth with courage, determination, and the knowledge that you possess the power to achieve great things. Fly, ambitious eagle, fly!

Chapter Summary

The third chapter of this book explores methods for achieving personal success. While reading this book cannot guarantee flawless application of these methods in your own life, it does provide an opportunity for you to engage in practical exercises. It is crucial to allocate ample time for reflection on the various topics presented to identify personal weaknesses. This introspection is pivotal in leading an organised life and attaining your goals. To assess your progress, consider the following questions:

1. Do I clearly understand what I am seeking to achieve?
2. Are my goals well-defined and specific?
3. Have I acquired the necessary skills and training to pursue my objectives effectively?
4. Am I organised in my approach, or do I tend to be disorganised when working towards my goals?
5. Do I have the perseverance and determination to overcome challenges and achieve my goals?
6. Have I learned how to harness smaller strengths to achieve significant power?
7. Am I willing to engage in creative endeavours, or does fear of failure hinder me from taking risks?

8. Have I established a well-structured schedule for attaining my goals, or am I rushing through the process?

9. When faced with challenges or failures, do I succumb to panic or remain focused on problem-solving and undeterred by fear?

Each of these questions will provide valuable insights into your journey. By carefully examining your responses, you can identify the reasons behind past failures and acquire problem-solving techniques. In certain instances, seeking guidance from a consultant, such as a psychologist, may be necessary, mainly if impulsive or timid behaviour stems from childhood experiences. Once you have methodically and comprehensively answered these questions and have actively addressed and improved upon your weaknesses through consistent practice, you will be on the path to success. It won't be long before you achieve your goals and become a commendable individual.

As your companion and friend, I eagerly await hearing your story. If this book has a transformative impact on your life, please share your experience with me. Together, we can build a vast network of successful individuals and serve as a source of motivation for those who may have lost hope. Welcome to the circle of successful people!

At the end of this book, I hope you find all the considerations and texts provided immensely valuable, allowing you to utilise them as a clinical guide. During moments of exhaustion, frustration, disappointment, or sadness, I encourage you to take hold of this book and immerse yourself in its contents. Within these pages, you will experience a transformative shift in your perspective on life, creation, and success.

Through this book, you will become acquainted with various forms of fulfilment and realise that success is not solely defined by monetary wealth. You will discover that you can experience profound joy without material possessions, surpassing the happiness of those who possess everything. This book serves to awaken your senses, expanding your vision and perception. It not only imparts techniques for enhancing your financial progress but also enriches your philosophical understanding, judgment, and perspective.

May you soar freely in the vast and beautiful sky of possibilities, fuelled by an unwavering desire to observe and explore all the world has to offer. Let nothing hinder your pursuit as you seize every opportunity that comes your way. You are a triumphant individual, firmly established in your own unique circumstances. Always remember and embrace this fact.

This book aims to provide you with the tools and insights needed to navigate the complexities of life, offering guidance and inspiration when you need it most. May it empower you to overcome challenges, transcend limitations, and unlock your true potential. Approach its wisdom with an open heart and a receptive mind, allowing its teachings to shape your journey towards personal and professional fulfilment.

As you turn the final page of this book, may you embark on a remarkable voyage enriched with newfound wisdom and a profound sense of purpose. May you navigate the seas of life with confidence, compassion, and resilience, always striving to impact the world around you positively. Remember, you possess the power to shape your own destiny and create a life filled with joy, meaning, and accomplishment.

May this book be your companion, providing solace and enlightenment whenever you encounter tribulations or seek guidance. Embrace its transformative power, and let it propel you towards a future where you transcend limitations and achieve greatness. The possibilities are boundless, and you possess the capacity to accomplish extraordinary things within you.

Go forth with courage, determination, and an unwavering belief in your abilities. Embrace the lessons of this book, internalise its teachings, and let it serve as a steadfast source of inspiration on your journey to personal and professional success. [2]

---

[2] **Dr Frankel**, in his renowned work "**Man's Search for Meaning**

Eric Fromm, in his book "To Have **or to Be.**"

Printed in Great Britain
by Amazon